"To a Creek Chub Bait"

A musky sat neath a musky weed,
Looking about for a luscious feed.
He saw some pickerel darting by,
And checked them over, with eager eye;
A gay little pike, with pajamas pink,
Came floating listlessly through the drink,
And a tough old jack, with a hard boiled face,
Scowled as he passed Mr. Musky's place.
Just then a plug, with a bright red head,
Came bouncing over the musky's bed.
He was out like a flash, he leaped with vim.
His jaws snapped shut. It was taps for him.
—Richard L. Sutton
from the 1935 Creek Chub catalog

Classic
Fishing
Lures
and Tackle

An Entertaining History of
Collectible Fishing Gear

Text by Eric L. Sorenson
Photography by Howard Lambert
Foreword by Ron Schara

A TOWN SQUARE BOOK

Voyageur Press

Frontispiece, main photo:
Goin' fishin'

A can of worms dug up from the backyard, a simple hook, a bamboo rod strung with fishing line, a single sinker, and a handful of wooden bobbers. The love of fishing starts at an early age and lasts a lifetime. Memorabilia owners: Pete Press and Guy Chambers.

Frontispiece, inset:
1932 South Bend catalog

Beautiful illustrations like this one of a boy and his stringer of sunfish were common advertising hooks on catalog covers during the first half of the twentieth century. The illustration suggests that purchasing a Bass-Oreno would guarantee an angler a successful day on the water.

Title page, main photo: **The bobber**

Ripples on the pond tell the fisherman or -woman that his quarry is below tugging on his line. With a red-white-and-blue color scheme, this bobber is as all-American as the sport of fishing.

Title page, inset:
"A fine catch for anyone"

Fishing postcards like this one of a female angler from the 1950s are insightful snapshots of the sport from past generations. The illustration and its caption suggest that female anglers were not always taken seriously by mainstream fishermen.

Opposite the contents: **Nice catch**

A 1930s photograph of a boy and an enormous largemouth bass represents the long-standing tradition of anglers posing for the camera with their prize catch.

On the endsheets:
Two Proud Anglers

Two proud anglers congratulate each other on their catch. Photograph courtesy of the Minnesota Historical Society.

4

Text copyright © 2000 by Eric L. Sorenson
Photographs copyright © 2000 by Howard Lambert

Edited by Margret Aldrich
Designed by Andrea Rud
Printed in Hong Kong

00   01   02   03   04   5   4   3   2   1

Library of Congress Cataloging-in-Publication Data
Sorenson, Eric L., 1966–
   Classic fishing lures and tackle : an entertaining history of collectible fishing gear / text by Eric L. Sorenson ; photography by Howard Lambert.
      p. cm.
"Town Square books."
Includes bibliographical references (p. 141).
   ISBN 0-89658-379-1
   1. Fishing lures—History. 2. Fishing tackle—History. 3. Fishing lures—Collectibles. 4. Fishing tackle—Collectibles. I. Lambert, Howard, 1947–
II. Title.

SH449 .S69 2000
688.7'91'075—dc21   00-027759

Distributed in Canada by Raincoast Books
9050 Shaughnessy Street, Vancouver, B.C. V6P 6E5

Published by Voyageur Press, Inc.
123 North Second Street, P.O. Box 338, Stillwater, MN 55082 U.S.A.
651-430-2210, fax 651-430-2211
books@voyageurpress.com
www.voyageurpress.com

Educators, fundraisers, premium and gift buyers, publicists, and marketing managers: Looking for creative products and new sales ideas? Voyageur Press books are available at special discounts when purchased in quantities, and special editions can be created to your specifications. For details contact the marketing department at 800-888-9653.

Dedication

Dedicated to my wife Gretchen Sorenson, my best friend and the love of my life, who understands, encourages, and supports my need to fish, write, and collect.

Eric L. Sorenson

Greetings from WINDOM, MINN.

Acknowledgments

The author wishes to thank the National Fishing Lure Collectors Club and the Old Reel Collectors Association.

Eric L. Sorenson

I would like to personally acknowledge the cooperation, generosity, and trust of all the collectors who contributed artifacts from their collections. I understand their passion for collecting things they love, and I am flattered that they allowed me to try to recreate a slice of time with their prized possessions. This book is dedicated to them, because without their help these images would not have been possible.

Howard Lambert

Above: **Postcard** *circa* **1950**

Contents

Foreword

Ron Schara

Most of us who fish don't think of our fishing stuff as "collectible."

We buy fishing lures, not to begin collecting, but to begin catching. That favorite fishing rod is not so much a collectible tool as a bending partner through our best and worst angling moments. That well-oiled reel is our intimate connection to the tasks of angling—the cast, the retrieve, the fight.

However, passing time eventually changes our view toward most things, including fishing tackle. History, they say, makes for collectibles, but I would add one more thing: the love of angling.

Most of us keep old fishing stuff around for reasons that go beyond their collectible value.

On my den wall, there's a well-used Mitchell fiberglass spinning rod. Its guide wraps are tattered and torn but none of the line guides are missing. The rod handle is well-soiled from countless days on countless river banks or from being held by dirtied hands fresh out of the worm can.

Those hands belonged to me, a teenage angler forty years ago.

The rod holds a cherished spot in my home. It was the first fishing rod I ever bought with my own money. I don't remember the fish we caught together but I haven't forgotten that the rod was a good and reliable fishing partner.

On a shelf below, there's an old fly reel with a name that has rusted away. I wish I knew what it was. While the reel might be a collectible model, it already is in my mind because my Uncle Ed once used that reel. Uncle Ed loved fly fishing for trout and he loved sharing his stories with me. He was my first fishing hero. When he died, I asked his widow if I could have that rusty reel. She thought it was worthless.

As I recall the retired lures hanging around my place, I'm surprised by the number. It's quite a collection, although we're not talking museum stuff here.

One lure is a green, sinking-model Rapala. I've kept that particular Rapala Countdown for two reasons.

First, the Rapala folks only made a few green-colored models to test the market.

Second, one day on Ontario's Lake of the Woods, a huge muskie

Facing page: **The strike**

An experienced collector could probably guess that this illustration of a largemouth bass leaping out of the water is from the 1930s by looking at the angler's tackle. Items such as the plug, heavy line, baitcasting rod, and wooden boat are clues in dating the artwork. The illustration was produced by Walter Haskell Hinton in 1937 for Sports Afield *magazine.*

inhaled that lure and gave me a severe case of muskie fever. When the battle was over and the fish lay beside the boat, I was faced with another dilemma.

Before me was the largest fish of my angling career.

My mind raced with a question: Should I consider keeping such a trophy?

Suddenly the green Rapala simplified the answer. The hooks popped free; the giant muskie swirled away and I was no longer tempted to keep the fish.

Good thing. The Ontario muskie season opened the next day.

Most of my retired lures are connected to big-fish-getaway stories. After all, who wants to remember lures lost to unseen snags or bad knots?

One of my collectibles is just a piece of a lure. It's a large saltwater hook as fat as a pinkie finger and tied to a crimped piece of 600-pound test cable. That's all that's left after a 1,000-pound Pacific blue marlin annihilated the lure by racing away with one-half mile of line before snapping the 600-pound test cable that held the rear hook. The rest of the lure is somewhere on the ocean floor off the Kona Coast of Hawaii.

Another favorite lure of mine is an old Heddon's River Runt. It's one of the first artificial lures I remember using as a boy fishing on the Mississippi River. It's also one of the first lures I remember losing.

To a fish.

It was not a tree limb. It was a fish. A fish strong and wise to the current's power. I was tactfully reeling when my fishing line parted with a dull snap.

There went the fish.

There went the lure.

There went my passion, my hopes, my dreams.

In life, there are no greater doldrums than those caused by the one that got away.

Lure and all.

Maybe this explains the birth of angling collectibles. This much I know, it is not born of fame nor riches. I suspect we anglers collect our fishing stuff to teach, to remind the world of angling's contributions to the well-being of humankind.

In that sense, collecting is a memorable catch of its own. Like a favorite fish mounted on our den wall, we yearn to have the pieces of our adventures in angling around to remember, to admire, to appreciate.

Lures, for example, may indeed be samples of the best assets of humankind.

Is a fishing lure not a package of hope and ingenuity? Is it not a symbol of our endless determination and imagination?

Do we quit when the fish are not biting?

Not me. Not you. We change lures.

About Ron Schara

As an entertaining and informed storyteller, Ron Schara's love for the outdoors is contagious. For more than thirty years, he has spread his enthusiasm for the waters and wilds of Minnesota to tens of thousands of readers and viewers, first as an award-winning outdoors journalist for the Minneapolis *Star Tribune* and now as the host of the television magazine programs *Minnesota Bound, Call of the Wild,* and *Backroads with Ron & Raven.*

The Punkinseed

This Heddon lure attracts the attention of a large walleye. Owner: Pete Press.

Introduction

Henry David Thoreau once wrote, "Time is just a river I go fishing in." If this statement is true for collectors, then they are wading upstream in it, into the past, casting for treasures to put in their creels. Each bend they reach in the river reveals new information and leads to further discovery. Occasionally collectors rest upon the bank and admire their catch. They look out over the gurgling eddies and pools and see the faces of inventors and builders of lures and reels wash across the pebbles and rocks. They wonder what secrets lie in the dark shadows and crevices below the surface of this river called time. At the end of the day they stop to enjoy a drink with friends, tell tales of the one that got away, and discuss strategies for improving their success. Just as fishing is an adventure, so too is collecting. No one ever knows if the next cast will produce the catch of a lifetime.

I became caught in the current of angling's past when I was a boy. I would spend countless hours sorting through the treasures in my grandfather's tackle box, admiring the lures, reels, and accessories he had accumulated over the years. I remember pointing to lures and asking him how many fish he had caught on them or how they worked. Sometimes he let me pick out a lure to add to my own tackle box, but I rarely used these lures for fear of losing them.

Later in life, I inherited most of the fishing tackle from both of my grandfathers. My curiosity about the origins of their rods, reels, and lures led me into that river called time as I searched for answers to my questions about these intriguing pieces of angling history. My searches led me down new paths, and soon I was buying other people's old lures and tackle. Before I knew it, I was a collector.

There are many factors that lead anglers into collecting old tackle and lures, such as an appreciation for fine artisanship or a curiosity for the odd and unique. However, the real draw is being able to reach out and touch pieces of the past, while learning about the people who contributed their sweat and ideas to shaping an industry. Those who motor out on the lake each weekend and toss baits at fish while never knowing who Hiram Leonard or George Snyder were are able to enjoy many aspects of fishing, but anglers who collect old fishing tackle open the door to a new plane. They take with them a greater understanding and appreciation for the sport, its tools, and the anglers who pushed forward its evolution.

Facing page: **"Fish and feel fit!"**
Slogans such as "Fish and feel fit," which appeared on South Bend's 1929 catalog cover, have long been important advertising tools for tackle companies. This slogan and accompanying illustration suggest anglers who fish with South Bend's lures and tackle experience a contagious euphoria of health and happiness.

Chapter 1

Rods

Main photo: **The romance of fly fishing**

Fly fishing's mystique lies as much in the beauty of a mountain stream, a perfect cast, and the ultimate catch as it does in the art of trout and salmon fishing equipment. The reel mounted on the rod was manufactured circa 1910 by the famous A. F. Meisselbach & Brother company of Newark, New Jersey, during the golden age of machine-made American fishing reels. The Horricks-Ibbotson rod was hand made in about 1920. Memorabilia owner: Pete Press.

Inset: **Postcard *circa* 1950**

What could be better than lazily drifting away a beautiful day with a friend on a north-woods lake? A pair of anglers are portrayed doing just that on this 1950s postcard.

1945 Montague advertisement

The Montague Rod and Reel Company was one of many tackle manufacturers that focused their efforts on building affordable, quality split-bamboo rods during the first half of the twentieth century.

Simply put, a fishing rod is a tool that extends an angler's reach. Whether it is a branch snapped from a tree or a graphite wand born from the wonders of space-age technology, the fishing rod is an instrument of sport built to bring an angler closer to his or her quarry. Through the centuries, this tool has evolved from its crude beginnings to its present form. Changes in anglers' needs and the application of available technology have shaped it and pulled it in various directions. Over time, as materials improved and production became easier, anglers continually asked more from the rod, requiring it not only to increase their range and decrease their chances of spooking fish, but also to fight fish and cast baits.

During this evolutionary process, some rods became cherished works of art, while others were discarded and forgotten as casualties—often because their designs were unreliable or eclipsed by technological advances—in the never-ending battle to build a better rod. For the collector, the artwork meticulously crafted by the skilled hands of the masters is the true prize. These rods stand as unforgettable measuring sticks along the evolutionary road. They endure the scrutiny of time and endear themselves to the hearts of collectors. Names such as Leonard, Payne, Edwards, and Thomas are synonymous with excellence. Because these builders created beautiful, finely tuned instruments, they set the standard by which the quality of a fishing rod is measured.

No one is certain exactly when anglers began using rods, but historians know the practice dates back thousands of years. It is evident through the study of ancient artwork that the Egyptians, Macedonians, Chinese, and Greeks used forms of the fishing rod, but the details concerning their contributions to rod technology are sketchy at best.

For as long as humans have tried to catch fish, they have searched for more efficient ways of doing it. The rod—along with the net, spear, and trap—was a logical tool, but the earliest rods were undoubtedly crude and awkward, with thick line made from vine and a hook fashioned from bone, shell, or wood.

The first rod builders probably struggled with some of the basic design challenges contemporary rod companies like Fenwick and Sage face in their technological development. When they built rods, factors such as length, strength, and feel affected their designs. Although most rods were considered multi-purpose until the 1800s, each fishing situation in fact required a different type of rod. To catch a large fish, an angler needed a strong, reliable rod. Catching smaller fish required a lighter rod with more feel. Rods needed the right amount of give to protect fragile line, but could not give so much that the rod itself would break. Of course, a thousand years ago, rod builders had a limited number of materials to choose from. They could only experiment with different types of wood in different sizes. Yet their work was the first step on the long road of experimentation that lead to the modern rod.

Multi-Piece Rods

The evolution of fishing-rod design crept slowly through the centuries until the 1800s, when new materials and machines of mass production opened the door to a wave of advancements in rod technology. Before the boom of the late nineteenth century, one of the first dramatic design innovations was the multi-piece rod.

The multi-piece rod extended an angler's reach two or three times the distance of a single-piece rod. Some rods incorporated a dozen or more pieces and measured as much as twenty feet (6 m) in length. The added length created a new challenge when it came time to land a fish. Before the use of reels, anglers could not simply yank fish in with these very long rods. They backed the rod in until they

Streamside

Trout fishing requires an angler who is patient, stealthy, and coordinated of hand and eye, as well as foot, when negotiating over and around slippery boulders in a swift, cold current. In addition, the angler must also be a bit of an entomologist and craftsperson. The reward for these virtues is sometimes a creel filled with delicious trout. Memorabilia owner: Pete Press.

could reach the line, then pulled the line and fish toward them. This may seem awkward and tiresome by today's standards, but it was a common practice a few hundred years ago. Amazingly, some European anglers still use this method, clinging to a tradition their ancestors started centuries ago. In North America, a few anglers still use cane poles, which at times require a similar technique.

In 1496, Dame Juliana Berners, the abbess of the Sopwell Priory in England, described in detail how to build a three-piece, two-section fly rod in the *Treatyse of Fysshynge wyth an Angle,* a chapter from the *Boke of St. Albans.* According to Berners, an angler built the butt section of the rod from hazel or rowan harvested during the winter. The woods were selected for their strength, light weight, and durability. To straighten the piece of wood, the builder tied it to a board and heated it in an oven until the smoke thoroughly dried it. The builder then burned the soft pith out with a hot, iron rod to hollow and evenly taper the inside. The finished section measured six feet (1.8 m) or more in length and had ferrules, hollow tubes of brass or iron, attached at either end. The top section, which also measured six feet (1.8 m) or more in length, was crafted from two pieces of wood. The lower part, made from green hazel, was spliced to an upper section made from blackthorn, crabtree, juniper, or medlar—woods that were strong and flexible, even when thinly tapered. The angler was able to compact the rod by carrying the upper section in the hollowed butt section.

The art of fly fishing

Fly fishing's artistic allure is exemplified in this fly fisherman's collection of tackle. The tackle shown here includes a Pflueger Golden West reel in mint condition. It is mounted on a South Bend Cross Custom Built rod, model 166. Memorabilia owner: Pete Press.

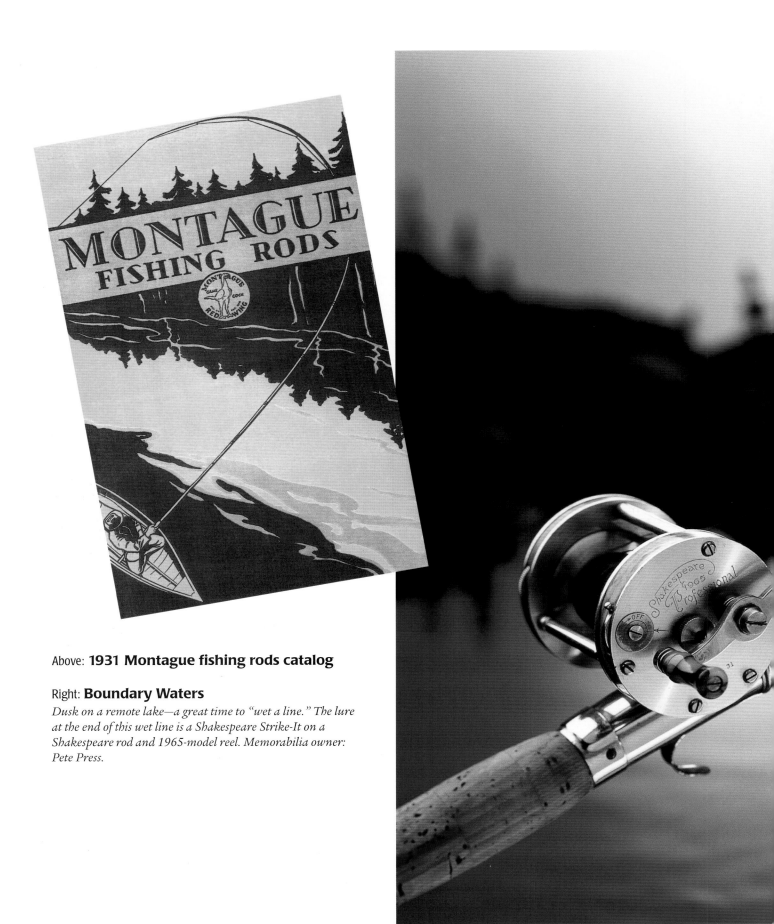

Above: **1931 Montague fishing rods catalog**

Right: **Boundary Waters**

Dusk on a remote lake—a great time to "wet a line." The lure at the end of this wet line is a Shakespeare Strike-It on a Shakespeare rod and 1965-model reel. Memorabilia owner: Pete Press.

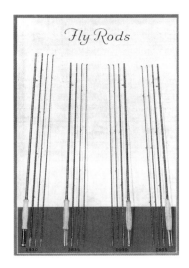

Fly Rods

The development of the multi-piece rod led to additional innovations in rod building. Anglers enjoyed new-found freedom with their extended reach, but they needed stronger and more efficient joints to hold their rod sections together. Ferrules, like those described by Berners, conjoined the sections of the earliest multi-piece rods. The butt end of one section fit inside the ferrule that was connected to the opposing piece to hold the sections together. Berners described adding a brass or iron ring that slipped over the connection to seal the joint. By the seventeenth century, rod makers were securing hollow metal sleeves crafted from brass, copper, silver, or German silver, around the wooden base of the connection to provide a better fit. In some cases, as Berners also notes in her writings, splices held the sections together. Rod builders commonly tied a string or leather thong around a splice to help strengthen the connection.

The period between the seventeenth and nineteenth centuries marked a transition from an emphasis on individual rod building to commercial rod production. Through the mid-1800s, however, individual anglers continued to shape the rod's development. For the average person, commercial rods were not available or affordable until the 1800s when mass production made them more accessible and inexpensive. Anglers could not just stop at the local sporting goods store and pick up a rod when they wanted to go fishing. It took weeks, even months, to build a good rod, and a large fish or accident could destroy all that hard work in the blink of an eye. Because of this, when anglers built their rods, they went to great lengths to use the best materials and the latest building techniques. They wanted to be sure that their handiwork could endure the everyday stresses of fishing; thus, they continually searched for ways to improve their rods' designs. Word of mouth carried innovations from angler to angler, but written instructions like Berners's also spread the word of advances in technology and design to individual anglers and, later, commercial builders.

Birth of Commercial Builders

In the same way it is impossible to say who built the first fishing rod, it is also unclear who first began making and then selling their rods. Documented work by commercial rod builders from Great Britain, such as Eaton & Deller, dates back to the early 1600s, and historians believe that colonial Americans built and sold rods around this time as well. However, the commercial fishing-rod trade probably began decades, if not centuries, before that. Although the details of the origins of commercial fishing-rod production are cloudy, the fact that early commercial builders were craftspeople who took pride in their work and strove to create better and more efficient tools for their customers is clear. Like today's rod builders, they experimented endlessly to come up with better products.

Early commercial builders focused on improving the multi-piece rod, which still had problems to overcome in the 1600s. Builders fought with creating better joints to hold sections together. The joints had to be reliable, but could not interfere with the performance of the rod. They experimented with various types of woods and with hollowing those woods out to make rods more flexible. They also strove to make long rods lighter and easier to carry.

By the 1600s, reels began appearing in Britain, which added new challenges to rod building. Rod makers now needed to develop clamps to hold the reel on the rod, and they had to design guides that would keep the rod and line together.

Commercial rod building, and the sport-tackle trade in general, did not really start to flourish until around the mid-1700s, and very few examples of rods built before that time survive today. During the 1800s, the industry came of age and moved into what collectors now recognize as the classic period of rod building.

One important factor that contributed to the explosion in the rod-building industry in the nineteenth century was access to exotic woods that were previously unavailable in Europe or the United States. British explorations to India, South America, and the Caribbean brought home superior tropical woods. Among the most popular in the rod-building trade were lancewood, a tough and elastic wood from Cuba and British Guiana; greenhart, a resilient, fine- to medium-textured wood from the bibiri tree in the West Indies and British Guiana; as well as wabasha, snakewood, paddlewood, and steelwood. These new discoveries allowed rod builders to create lighter, stronger, and more resilient rods. Although numerous tropical woods played roles in the rod-building evolution, bamboo became the most important import, because of its light weight and superior strength. The arrival of this tropical grass on the rod-building scene eventually catapulted American rod builders into the spotlight and marked the beginning of a new age in sport angling.

Split-Cane Rods

Until the nineteenth century, British rod builders dominated the commercial trade. Anglers considered the British work far superior to and more innovative than the rods built by Americans. Their dominance came to an end when American rod builders began producing the split-cane bamboo rod, which has become the sparkling gem of rods in the eyes of collectors. Although the British experimented with split-cane rods in the late 1700s and early 1800s, it was not until the mid- to late nineteenth century that the technique began to emerge in the United States and gain popularity in the commercial trade.

South Bend split-bamboo baitcasting rods

South Bend grew to become one of the largest tackle manufacturers in North America—in part, by establishing a reputation for meeting the average angler's needs. The copy on this page from a 1929 catalog emphasizes that South Bend's rods were well built, yet carried a reasonable price tag, which was important to the blue-collar workers that accounted for a solid share of the company's business. The slogan "There's a South Bend Rod for Every Kind of Fishing," underscores the company's inclusive image and the variety of products it sold.

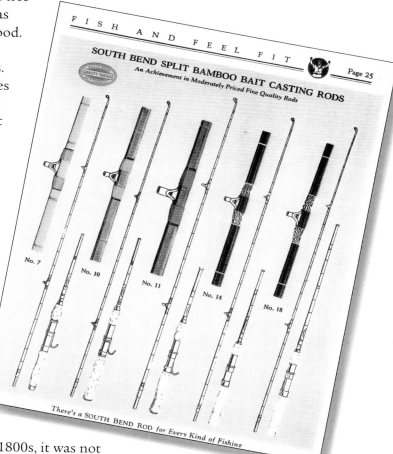

FISH AND FEEL FIT

SOUTH BEND SPLIT BAMBOO BAIT CASTING RODS
An Achievement in Moderately Priced Fine Quality Rods

Page 25

No. 7   No. 10   No. 11   No. 14   No. 18

There's a SOUTH BEND ROD for Every Kind of Fishing

Angling for bass

The bass is notorious for putting up a ferocious fight, but he is no match for tough tackle. This reel is an Eli model made by the Wm. H. Talbot Reel Company of Nevada, Missouri. The split-bamboo rod was made by James Heddon & Sons of Dowagiac, Michigan. The bass lure on the line is a Baby Seagull made by the Moonlight Bait Company of Paw Paw, Michigan. These items are from the collection of Pete Press. The handmade tackle box and other lures are from the collection of Guy Chambers. Included here is a mint-condition Bass-Oreno plug and its original box circa 1920. Made by the renowned South Bend Bait Company of South Bend, Indiana, the Bass-Oreno was "the bait that truly has a wobbling motion."

As its name implies, the process of building a split-cane rod involves splitting the bamboo's outer layer into even strips along the grain. Builders first used three- or four-strip construction before experimenting with six- and eight-strip designs. Eventually, the six-strip style became the norm. Once the strips are cut, the builder meticulously shaves each into a thin, triangular shape. The strips are glued together, forming a hexagonal outer edge. The builder then cuts the blank to its final taper. During the 1800s, rod makers often rounded the outer edges of their rods. Some builders wrapped thread intermittently around the rod to help hold the glued strips together. The final product was a rod that outperformed nearly every type previously produced, because bamboo offered a combination of light weight, strength, feel, and shorter length that other rod materials could not match.

According to tackle historians, Samuel Phillippe and his son Solon of Easton, Pennsylvania, were the first rod builders in America to make rod sections out of split-cane bamboo. Samuel first experimented with splitting bamboo in the 1840s. He and Solon worked

with three- and four-strip construction before settling on a six-strip design. However, Charles F. Murphy of Newark, New Jersey, a friend of the Phillippes, built the first rods made entirely with six-strip sections during the early 1860s. Murphy was also the first commercial producer of split-cane rods and helped to spawn the wave of popularity in split-cane construction.

Despite the work by the Phillippes and Murphy, the major force behind the popularization of the split-cane rod was a Bangor, Maine, rod builder named Hiram Lewis Leonard. Leonard built his first rod out of ash and lancewood in 1871. Soon afterward, he started experimenting with bamboo and built his first split-cane rod after receiving a request from sporting goods retailer Bradford & Anthony of Boston. In his early experimentation with split-cane, Leonard used a four-strip design, but after a short time he modified his technique and started producing rods in the familiar six-strip style.

Leonard built many rods of legendary quality during his career. Among them were the Catskill trout rods. Built with German-silver reel seats and butt caps, and cigar-shaped grips, they helped Leonard earn the title of father of the modern fly rod.

Despite the high quality of his fishing rods, Leonard's commercial success was rooted in a revolutionary invention called the power beveler, which he developed around 1876. His invention cut each blank to a uniform size and allowed him to produce dozens of blanks in little time. Although the power beveler cut down on the time and money Leonard spent building rods, his rods were by no means inexpensive. In 1877, anglers could purchase his three-piece, seventeen-foot (5.2-m) salmon rod for fifty dollars, a monumental price for the average late-nineteenth-century angler. Leonard tried to keep his power beveler under wraps, but other rod manufacturers discovered his secret and began mass producing split-cane rods in a similar manner.

In 1881, Leonard moved the H. L. Leonard Rod Company to Central Valley, New York, where it still operates today. The move boosted Leonard's business because it allowed him to establish important connections with New York City tackle dealers. Leonard's rod-building career spanned more than thirty years and ended with his death in 1907 in Central Valley. His factory never stopped producing high-quality split-cane rods, however. Partner Thomas Mills took over the company after Leonard's death, and his descendants continued to operate the business for many decades. The SC Johnson Wax Company of Racine, Wisconsin, bought the company in 1978.

"Outstanding Steel Rods"

During the late 1930s and early 1940s, steel rods began competing with split-bamboo rods for anglers' attention. Though their popularity lasted just a few decades, steel rods gained acceptance because they were more durable than split bamboo and were easier and cheaper for tackle companies to produce. This advertisement from a 1943 Dave Cook Sporting Goods Company catalog lists both steel and split-bamboo rods, but the emphasis on steel rods reflects the popularity of this new technology during the middle decades of the twentieth century.

Other now-classic commercial builders followed in Leonard's footsteps during the late 1800s and through the turn of the century. Some, such as Hiram and Loman Hawes (Leonard's nephews), Edward F. Payne, Fred E. Thomas, and Eustice W. Edwards, also came from Bangor and spent time working for Leonard. They learned the craft of building high-quality split-cane rods from this pioneer, then went on to make their own marks in rod-building history. Other notable builders during this period included Charles F. Orvis and Thomas Chubb of Vermont, and George Varney from New York.

Neither American nor British anglers instantly accepted split-cane rods, although anglers in the United States were much quicker to embrace bamboo than the English. When commercial split-cane rods first appeared in the 1870s, anglers were reluctant to abandon more traditional rod-building materials. They also knew split-cane rod building was a new and imperfect art. Manufacturers still had to overcome problems like finding the right waterproof glues to adhere to bamboo. They also worked at creating better ferrules and developing more efficient milling techniques. By the mid-1880s, though, rod makers had solved most of these problems and the split-cane rod industry started to flourish.

Many of the early commercial rods were exquisite and costly, but some manufacturers, like the Charles F. Orvis Company of Manchester, Vermont, used mass-production techniques to create less expensive rods that were more affordable to the average angler. Orvis built good rods that sold for considerably less than a Leonard rod. The South Bend Bait Company of South Bend, Indiana; James Heddon & Sons of Dowagiac, Michigan; the Shakespeare Company of Kalamazoo, Michigan; the Montague Rod and Reel Company of Montague City, Massachusetts; and other companies followed suit in the early 1900s, producing affordable, yet quality, split-cane rods.

By the end of the nineteenth century and into the early twentieth century, the commercial split-cane rod became a staple in American angling, as consumers came to recognize the benefits of using the rods and manufacturers began to flood the market. The first half of the 1900s was a prosperous period for talented builders such as Harold "Pinky" Gillum, Paul H. Young, Lyle Dickerson, William Taylor, Omar Needham, Morris Kushner, Lew Stoner, and Doug Merrick of the R. L. Winston Rod Company in San Francisco; Edwin Powell and Tony Maslan of the E. C. Powell Rod Company in Marysville, California; Wesley Jordan of the Cross Rod Company of Lynn, Massachusetts, and Orvis; and Everett Garrison, Fred Divine, and Goodwin Granger, who were best known for their work as independent rod builders. These builders and others created exceptional, unforgettable rods that collectors cherish today.

To the novice who finds a split-cane bamboo rod in their grandfather's basement or at some garage sale and thinks they have discovered a treasure, the reality might be somewhat disheartening. Although that antique split-cane rod is undoubtedly a beautiful

NO
BREAK
TO A
UTK
FISHING
ROD

piece of fishing memorabilia, it may not have much monetary value. Many people are shocked when they learn that their split-cane treasure is worth less than fifty dollars.

Part of the confusion likely results from the price of a modern split-cane rod, which is usually a substantial investment. In contrast, in the first half of the 1900s, low- to mid-quality split-cane rods were readily available and quite inexpensive. To draw an analogy, a 1935 Ford and a 1935 Cadillac are both unique automobiles because they are old. However, the difference in quality between an affordable Ford and a luxury Cadillac polarizes their collectible values. Just as an old Ford is easier to find and less expensive to purchase than a classic Cadillac, collectors are much more likely to find an inexpensive split-cane rod tucked away in their grandfather's garage than they are an expensive, handmade rod.

During the late 1800s, Calcutta cane from India was the wood of choice for split-cane rod builders. But in the early 1900s, Tonkin cane from China displaced Calcutta as the ideal split-cane rod material. The harder, more resilient Tonkin cane improved the casting distance and the sensitivity of rods. By the 1950s, Tonkin cane became quite difficult to come by after an embargo on trade with communist China went into effect. The severing of the supply of Tonkin cane forced some split-cane builders to close their shops.

Although factors such as the embargo on Tonkin cane and the emergence of new rod-building materials like steel, fiberglass, and graphite during the '50s, '60s, and '70s dealt the split-cane rod a series of blows, its popularity waned but never died. Today, split-cane rods continue to enjoy a loyal following, and a number of large and small commercial sources still produce them. Many split-cane rod enthusiasts, however, choose to build their own rods, continuing the tradition forged by those classic American artisans in the late nineteenth and early twentieth centuries. Numerous books and classes on the topic are available, making it fairly easy for beginners to get started. Other anglers prefer using antique split-cane rods to fully experience the quality and craftsmanship that was so much a part of the fishing rod's evolution.

"From American Sports Come American Heroes!"

A 1944 Heddon advertisement for rods and lures typified tackle companies' use of patriotism to help sell products during World War II. Both split-bamboo and steel rods are listed in the ad, but Heddon's "Pal" steel rods received top billing, illustrating the rod-building industry's move away from split-bamboo production during the 1940s.

Baitcasting Rods

The development of the split-cane rod was not the only revolutionary innovation in rod technology during the nineteenth century. The second major design change that swept across the industry was the improvement of the casting efficiency of the rod and reel.

Although tackle manufacturers built high-quality rods and reels during the mid-1800s, no one had figured out a way of effectively

linking them to cast baits. In the 1880s, rod builder Dr. James Henshall of Kentucky introduced a new breed of fishing rod called the Henshall rod, which the Orvis Company manufactured. His design aimed at adapting the rod to the multiplying reel in order to improve the rod's baitcasting efficiency. His rod was relatively short, measuring eight feet, three inches (2.5 m), and weighed less than most rods on the market, which made it easier to handle.

The Henshall rod proved an instant success, but its popularity did not last long. A few years after its introduction, a shorter, spilt-cane baitcasting rod called the Chicago rod pushed the Henshall rod out of the spotlight. Like Henshall, James M. Clark of Illinois designed his Chicago rod specifically for casting baits. But Clark went a step further than Henshall, building a rod that measured just six feet (1.8 m) in length, which, at the time, was a drastic departure in rod design. The Chicago rod eventually became a model other rod makers imitated, setting the standard for baitcasting rods.

It is safe to say the introduction of both the Henshall and Chicago rods was one of the most dramatic advances in the evolution of fishing tackle. Not only did these rods finally make it easy for anglers to cast baits effectively, they also helped launch the lure industry. Following the Chicago rod's introduction, increasing numbers of lure manufacturers appeared, as everyone from big businesses to basement-based builders tried to cash in on the growing popularity of baitcasting.

The ice-fishing house

Ice fishing requires true dedication. The ice fisherman and -woman must brave the elements to while away the hours in the seclusion of this winter home away from home. Here is ice-fishing equipment from the 1920s and 1930s, including a handmade wooden rod, two steel rods and reels made by Stubby, scoops, auger, sled, snowshoes, a 1933 copy of National Sportsman *magazine, and a 1920s-model Coleman lantern with hand pump. The heated minnow bucket was an especially creative invention: Inside the insulated metal bucket was a miniature kerosene lantern that kept the water from freezing and the minnows fresh for deep-winter fishing. Memorabilia owner: Pete Press.*

New Materials

In the mid-1930s, Dr. Glen Havens of National City, California, introduced a new, controversial material known as fiberglass to the fishing world when he built the first fiberglass rod, and he subsequently turned the rod-building industry on end. Some anglers embraced fiberglass as superior to bamboo as rod-building material, while others cursed it as a blight on the industry. In many cases, fiberglass provided anglers with a lighter, more durable rod for a fraction of the cost of a quality split-cane rod. It also required very little care. For the average angler, it was a welcome advancement in rod technology. Fiberglass was also an improvement for some rod manufacturers, who could produce high numbers of rods for less money than it cost to make split-cane rods. The fiberglass rod's surge in popularity, along with the introduction of the short-lived steel rod, put many split-cane rod builders out of business or forced them to switch to fiberglass or steel production.

It took some time for fiberglass rods to catch on, however. The 1940s saw the birth of the fiberglass rod market, but early on, manufacturers struggled with perfecting the technology. The first fiberglass rods contained a wooden core. Later, manufacturers introduced rods of solid fiberglass and then hollow fiberglass. The real boom started when Shakespeare introduced its Howald process rods in 1946, with a hollow, tapered blank.

The tubular design continues in production today, although the fiberglass rod's popularity has fizzled. Its moment in the limelight was rather brief in the scheme of rod evolution—the peak of its popularity lasted just a few short decades, before a revolutionary new material called graphite jumped to the forefront of rod technology.

The graphite rod made its debut in the early 1970s. The Fenwick Rod Company of Spirit Lake, Iowa, played a key role in helping to popularize this new material in the early years, and it remains one of the predominant graphite rod builders. As happened with the arrival of fiberglass, purists bitterly chastised the new material, but it did not take long for graphite to claim its place at the top of the rod market's pedestal. Graphite rods were lighter, smaller in diameter, more flexible, and stronger than fiberglass, and they added five to ten yards (4.5–9 m) to the distance of casts. Anglers could not resist this superior material's unmatched performance.

Today, a visit to any sporting goods store reveals that the majority of rods on the market are of graphite construction. However, some anglers, fly fishermen in particular, still prefer split-bamboo rods, whether it be for sentimental reasons or because they favor the artisanship and unique performance of handmade split-bamboo rods.

Gephart advertisement

Catchy slogans have always played an important role in tackle manufacturers' advertisements. Though it might have worked in the 1940s for the Gephart Manufacturing Company of Chicago, Illinois, "Get hep to Gep" would probably not sell many rods in today's marketplace.

Collectibles

Most collectors of fishing rods focus on split-bamboo rods built during the late 1800s through the mid-1900s. However, early fiberglass rods are starting to gain some popularity as collectibles. Handmade split-cane rods built by classic craftspeople, such as those mentioned earlier in this chapter, tend to command the highest prices, because their work demonstrates a quality and beauty that surpasses the majority of the factory-built rods. This does not mean that inexpensive split-bamboo rods have no place in the world of collectibles. In fact, some collectors focus primarily on these models.

Values of split-cane rods vary depending on the scarcity and condition of the rods. A rod may be scarce, but if it was repaired, damaged, or altered, the price drops significantly. Even minor wear or seemingly insignificant damage can dramatically affect a rod's value.

Although collectors can buy split-cane rods from a wide variety of sources, ranging from flea market vendors to Internet sites, it is usually best (especially for beginners) to buy rods from reputable sources. Experienced collectors are aware that counterfeit rods are on the market and that mail order or Internet sources may misrepresent a rod's condition. A good source for information about trustworthy dealers is the National Fishing Lure Collectors Club.

The split-bamboo rod's popularity as a collectible continues to increase, which suggests that values will remain high for years to come. While it is uncertain which of today's rods will become collectibles in the future, contemporary, handmade split-cane rods will probably join the ranks of collectibles as well.

Graphite rods, on the other hand, could likely have limited attraction as collectibles, because they lack the handmade expression found in quality split-cane rods. However, limited additions, prototypes, and early models of graphite rods may hold some value in the decades to come.

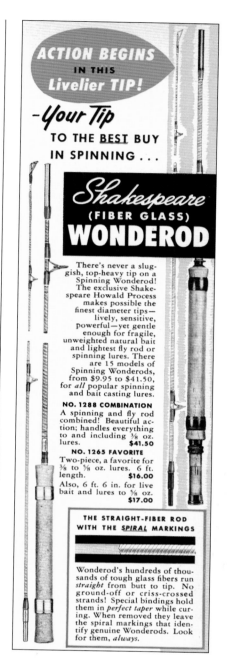

Wonderod

Shakespeare's Wonderod revolutionized the tackle industry by helping to popularize the use of fiberglass in rod construction. The company's Howald Process design was a technological breakthrough that dealt split-bamboo rods a devastating blow.

Chapter 2

Reels

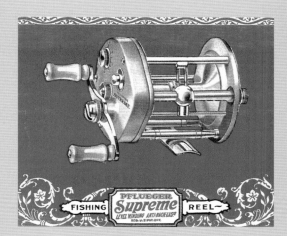

Main photo: **Daybreak**

The cedar strip canoe silently glides through shallow water to a favorite fishing hole. The kerosene lantern illuminates the fishing gear, which includes a Hurdcaster rod and reel and a Shannon Twin-Spin spoon. From the collection of Bud Snyder.

Inset: **Pflueger Supreme reel**

The Pflueger Supreme was one of the most popular baitcasting reels in North America during the 1920s and 1930s. It offered anglers features such as reliable level-wind and anti-backlash mechanisms, easy maintenance, and the quality and dependability that came with purchasing a Pflueger product.

To the modern angler, the rod and reel are a team that works hand in hand to accomplish the common goal of catching fish. Apart, they are mere pieces of fishing equipment, but together they form a powerful union that has endured and evolved for more than two centuries. It is possible to catch fish without a reel, but long ago anglers discovered that the rod was a much more effective tool when used in combination with a reel. Of course, the benefit a reel provides varies according to the type of job an angler requires it to perform. A fly fisherman or -woman may need it to do nothing more than hold line, while a muskie angler wants more, asking it to both throw line out across the water and fight fish. A reel plays the role of receptacle, casting tool, and brake—sometimes in combination, other times separately. The day-to-day demands placed on a reel punish it and push it to its limits of strength and function. Only a precision-crafted piece of machinery survives such demands through years of use, and those refined examples of engineering, produced by the masters of the trade, are the reels collectors hold in highest esteem.

Asking who invented the reel is like asking who invented the wheel. It is impossible to credit any one person with such an achievement. What historians do know, however, is that the act of using a stick to hold and carry fishing line is an ancient practice. Many cultures, including the Egyptians and Native Americans, used such a tool thousands of years ago, but these primitive reels did not attach to rods nor were they used to actually fish. Historians point to the Chinese as the first culture to place a reel on a rod and use the combination to fish. Although it is not certain exactly when this monumental act first took place, Chinese artwork from the twelfth century's Sung Dynasty portrays anglers using the rod and reel together.

1950s postcard

This postcard illustration depicts anglers fishing for salmon at Oregon's Rogue River.

Halfway around the world in Europe, the reel emerged somewhere around the seventeenth century. The first English literary reference to the reel, or winch as it was then called, appeared in Thomas Barker's book, *The Art of Angling*, published in 1651. The winch's popularity increased dramatically in Europe during the 1700s as growing numbers of anglers discovered its value in fighting large game fish like northern pike and salmon.

Early on, builders made their reels entirely from wood. Domestic woods such as cherry, oak, and walnut dominated the trade until reel makers gained access to imports like mahogany and rosewood. The first reels were of single-action, closed-end design. Wooden pillars connected the end plates, and a metal screw or latch held the spindle and drum in place. Because wood wore so poorly, reel makers eventually replaced wooden moving parts with those made from iron or brass.

Despite the reel's growing popularity as an effective fishing tool

Shaker rod and reel

This fishing relic was hand-fashioned from wood by Shaker craftspeople circa *the early nineteenth century. Owner: Jim Meyer.*

Above: **Scottish salmon reels**

These uniquely appealing reels of wood, brass, and steel have stood the test of time. Memorabilia owner: Frank Miller.

Facing page: **Nottingham reels**

This reel style, first produced in 1830, was a traditional English favorite for decades and is still being produced. Pictured along with these Nottingham reels is a lancewood rod with double ferrules. From the collections of Frank Miller and Pete Press.

in the 1700s, anglers did not universally accept this new technology. Fly fishermen and others who pursued smaller fish shied away from the winch. It was the angler who went after larger species who embraced the reel as a helpful fighting tool during its infancy.

One of the first notable advancements in reel technology was the multiplying reel, which emerged in Britain during the 1770s. The identity of the multiplier's inventor is a mystery, but the design its creator left behind remains an integral part of contemporary reel construction. The multiplying reel allowed anglers to take line in more quickly, because it used gears to increase the ratio between the number of times the handle turned and the rate at which the spool rotated, producing ratios of 2:1, 3:1, 4:1, and more.

Although the English invented and used the multiplier, they did not care for its design very much. They disliked the complex gear system because they felt it added unnecessary complication to the reel. They instead preferred to stick with the simpler single-action or center-pin design. This led to the birth of the Nottingham reel in the 1830s, which became the English reel of choice and remained so well into the 1900s. The Nottingham's two-piece design featured a wooden spool and brass or silver hardware. A few manufacturers still

produce such reels, including Lewtham Engineering of England and Peetz Tackle LTD of British Columbia, which manufacture wooden center-pin reels on a limited basis.

In America, anglers preferred the multiplying reel over the center-pin. It is not clear why Americans gravitated toward the multiplier. Maybe the American watchmakers who would later adapt and popularize the craft of reel making enjoyed the challenge offered by the multiplier's complex gear systems. Whatever the reason, as sport fishing grew in America, reel makers embraced the multiplier's technology and nourished its growth until it blossomed into the classic American reel.

Early American Reels

While fishing flourished as a sport in Britain during the eighteenth century, it had not yet caught on in America. Fishing was considered a hobby, and early Americans did not have much free time—they were too busy fighting for freedom and carving out a new life in a new land. The few Americans who did fish brought reels with them from Europe or bought imported British reels. So as the popularity of fishing began to grow in the United States during the early 1800s and American craftspeople began to build reels, the natural course was to use existing technology as a blueprint. Both the center-pin and multiplying designs were available, but American reel makers eventually gravitated toward the multiplier.

The first reel maker of note in the United States was a Paris, Kentucky, watchmaker named George Snyder. Although he did not invent the multiplying reel, Snyder influenced its design more than any other reel maker and helped launch its rise in popularity in the United States. In the early decades of the nineteenth century, Snyder applied his precision watchmaking skills toward building a better reel. The result was the first multiplying reel that allowed an angler to cast from the reel. His work spawned the school of Kentucky reel design. Anglers revered his quadruple multiplying reels for the unmatched smoothness of the spool rotation, which became a trademark of Kentucky reels.

Other Kentucky watchmakers followed Snyder's lead into reel making. Brothers Benjamin and Jonathan Meek of Frankfort, who improved on gear design and contributed to the development of the drag, hold claim to the first commercial production of the Kentucky reel. Benjamin Meek later manufactured the now-famous Blue Grass baitcasting reels with his two sons. Later, other Kentucky-based builders like Benjamin C. Milam of Frankfort, who went into business with Benjamin Meek for a time, James L. Sage, George W. Gayle, Frank Fullilove, James Deally, and Thomas Dalton made their mark with the Kentucky reel. By the mid-1800s, Kentucky reel makers had firmly established their tradition of high-quality products. Unfortunately, they rarely patented their designs, so collectors have a hard time identifying when specific innovations occurred.

While the Kentucky reel makers were busy building their tradition, reel makers in the northeastern United States were hard at work establishing their own school of reel design, which became known as the New York reel. Although the two types of reels were similar in both design and quality, there were some distinct differences. The most notable was the New York builders' use of a counterbalance on the crank. This feature, possibly developed by John C. Conroy of New York City in the 1830s, became a trademark of the New York reel. The balanced crank, with a handle on one end and a weight on the other, improved the reel's casting performance by adding momentum to the spool. It also decreased the wear on the ends of the spool shaft, giving the reel a longer life. The New York reels commonly used a 2:1 gear ratio and tended to be larger than their Kentucky counterparts. The size difference was a product of surfcasting, which was done on the East coast and required a larger, heavier reel.

Other notable builders from New York and the East Coast during this period included A. B. Shipley of Philadelphia, and John Krider, Andrew Clerk, and J. B. Crook of New York. Unlike their peers in Kentucky, northeastern reel makers were more diligent about patenting their designs. Because a fire in 1836 destroyed many of America's early patents, it is not certain who received the first patent for a fishing reel. The oldest surviving patent was granted to John A. Baily of Jersey City, New Jersey, in 1856. His patent was not for a reel, but for a part of the reel, protecting his design of a free spool device. William Billinghurst of New York received the first patent for a reel frame in 1859. His single-action reel with a brass-wire skeleton frame allowed fragile silk line to dry quickly, and it weighed significantly less than other reels on the market. Of course many patents followed, and their trail is an important research tool for tracing the progression of specific innovations in reel design.

For collectors, identifying these early American reels often requires significant detective work. They must pore over old patents, letters, and literature as they attempt to discover when specific models were built. In some cases, manufacturers stamped their company name or patent number on the reel, but more commonly a store name or a model number was the only identifying mark. However, discovering who made one of these early American reels is easy compared to the task of actually finding one. Dedicated collectors continue to search, though, hoping to stumble upon one of these rare gems, which remain among the most highly prized of all fishing collectibles. Their beauty and exceptional quality express the time and effort nineteenth-century craftspeople spent trying to perfect reel technology, and collectors long to own samples of their endeavors.

Continuing Traditions

Following the infancy of the American reel in the early to mid-1800s, the commercial reel market began to grow and mature in the second half of the century. Increasing numbers of builders joined the ranks.

Above: **"Built like a watch"**

The William Shakespeare Jr. Company established a reputation as a builder of affordable, precision reels during the first half of the twentieth century. The company's slogan, "Honor Built and Honor Sold," represented its commitment to excellence. Anglers who purchased a reel from this 1924 Shakespeare catalog knew they were buying one of the best products on the market.

Right: **The Kentucky Reel**

With its origins in the early 1800s, the school of Kentucky reel design played an influential role in reel development. Owner: Pete Press.

They used technological advances in manufacturing to shift commercial production from handmade models to machine-made, hand-assembled reels. Builders took major strides forward, improving on existing ideas while also producing new reel designs.

One of the first important inventions of the second half of the nineteenth century was the level-wind mechanism. Before the development of the level-wind reel, anglers guided the line with their fingers as they turned the crank to evenly distribute it across the spool. The level-wind mechanism was a loop or grooved shaft that moved back and forth across the spool as an angler reeled in the line, keeping the line level. Mark S. Palmer of New Bedford, Massachusetts, received the first patent for a level-wind device in 1860. The basic design behind his grooved-shaft, level-wind mechanism continues in production today on baitcasting and trolling reels. Other reel makers patented various versions of the level-wind device in the late 1800s, but a few decades passed before it was a common feature on commercial reels. The Wheeler & McGregor Company of Milwaukee, Wisconsin, produced the first commercial reel with the level-wind mechanism, when it introduced its Milwaukee reel in the 1890s. William Shakespeare Jr. of Kalamazoo, Michigan, who received his first reel patent in 1897, later popularized the commercial production of level-wind reels.

Another advancement of the last half of the nineteenth century was the use of brakes on multiplying reels. Snyder and other early reel makers used braking devices on their reels to stop fish from pulling line off the reel, but until the 1860s, the only tool anglers had to control the spool when casting line was their thumb. In 1864, Andrew Dougherty of Brooklyn, New York, received the first patent for the spool brake. His thumb-operated mechanism prevented the spool from spinning at the end of a cast, which cut down on the line tangles that accompany spool overrun. Reel makers began incorporating the brake into the design of baitcasting reels in the late 1800s. Since then, brake technology has come a long way, but despite more than a century of development, most serious anglers agree that the majority of the braking devices produced through the years have not matched the braking efficiency and control of the human thumb.

Through the mid-1800s, most reel makers did not design reels with specific types of fishing in mind, other than to adjust the size of the reel to match the size of the fish an angler wanted to pursue. That trend changed in the 1870s when Charles F. Orvis of Manchester, Vermont, introduced his revolutionary Orvis Trout Reel, designed specifically for fly fishing. Orvis received patent number

Automatic reels

Although it enjoyed some success, the automatic fly reel's popularity was limited. Major tackle manufacturers such as Heddon, South Bend, Pflueger, and Shakespeare each issued automatic reels, but many anglers shied away from the design, because the reels were heavy and could not be used to fight fish.

150,883 in 1874 for what anglers today recognize as the traditional fly-reel design. His single-action reel was both a step forward and a step backward in reel technology, because he created a new breed of reels while dramatically simplifying the mechanics of the reel. Instead of the complex gear mechanisms common to the American multiplying reel, Orvis simply designed a narrow spool that used the line to increase the retrieval rate. Orvis also perforated the sides and spool to reduce the weight of the reel and to allow line to dry more quickly. This cut down on the problems of mildew and rot that accompanied the use of silk lines. The reel mounted upright on the rod, marking a departure from previously produced fly reels. The ingenious first model came with a black-walnut box and sold for only $2.50.

Although Orvis's reel launched a new trend in reel making, he does not deserve all the credit. Other reel makers like Billinghurst, who had earlier experimented with ways to reduce the weight of the reel and improve its line-drying efficiency, influenced his design.

Orvis built his Trout Reel with a new alloy called nickel-plated brass, but reel makers, including Orvis, experimented with other materials during the mid- to late 1800s, as they strove to improve design. A few builders attempted to use aluminum, but technology had not advanced far enough to make it a practical reel material. It would have to wait until the twentieth century to make its mark in reel construction.

One of the first attempts at incorporating vulcanite, or hard rubber, in reel design was patented by New York dentist Alonzo Fowler in 1872. Fowler wanted to reduce the weight of the reel, so he used the lightweight, hard rubber he used in making dentures to build his Gem reel. Unfortunately, Fowler's hard-rubber reel proved to be too fragile to withstand the stresses of fishing, but the idea behind his single-action, lightweight reel reflected the trend in reel building that led to the design of the Orvis Trout Reel. In fact, Orvis's original patent called for the use of rubber for his reel, although it did not restrict him to rubber. While he saw the possibilities rubber had in reel building, Orvis did not use it in his Trout Reel, because the material still had problems to overcome. As Fowler had discovered, thin, hard rubber was still too fragile and unreliable to make an effective reel-building material.

Orvis's reel sparked other builders to search for ways to improve the single-action fly reel. Although he did not invent the raised-pillar reel, Francais J. Philbrook of Bangor, Maine, did receive the first patent for the design in 1877. He then assigned the patent to rod maker Hiram Leonard, who marketed and sold Philbrook's reels. Philbrook's raised-pillar design offset the crossbars, placing them outside the spool, which increased the line capacity without increasing the weight of the reel. The raised-pillar design was not a monumental improvement to the reel, but it was an advancement that grabbed the attention of other builders, and many copied it.

In 1880, Francis A. Loomis of Onodaga, New York, received the

The Orvis Trout Reel

Charles F. Orvis altered the course of reel building when he patented his Trout Reel in 1874. His single-action reel, which featured a narrow spool with perforated sides, was built specifically for fly fishing. The introduction of the Trout Reel prompted other builders to take more creative approaches to designing reels.

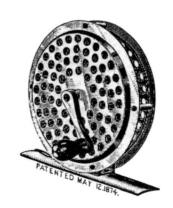

first patent for the automatic reel, a more dramatic innovation in fly-reel design. Through a spring-loaded mechanism, the automatic reel allowed an angler to take in slack line by simply pushing a lever. Although many companies produced automatic reels through the years, the design achieved only a limited following. Some anglers were annoyed that the reel's line retrieval rate was unreliable, while other anglers stayed away from the automatic reel because it provided no help in fighting a fish. Automatics were also heavy and had limited line capacity.

Among the most significant contributors to reel design in the late 1800s was the vom Hofe family. The family's tradition of reel making started with Frederick vom Hofe, who immigrated to New York from Austria in 1840. Frederick vom Hofe produced high-quality reels and passed the art on to his sons, Edward and Julius. Although Julius produced some exceptional reels during his career, it was Edward who went on to build many of the finest fishing reels anyone has ever made.

In 1867, at the age of twenty-one, Edward originated Edward vom Hofe & Company of New York City. Constantly striving to build a better reel, he made numerous design improvements, most notably to the click, drag, and gear systems, and was also one of the first reel makers to successfully incorporate hard rubber into reel design. The result of these innovations is a substantial list of reels whose quality may never be surpassed. Trout and salmon models of both single and double action, like the

A stormy night on Lake Superior

When fishing was slow for commercial fishermen, they would charter their boats for sport fishing. Fishing on the great freshwater sea required unique tackle that would reach the depths needed to angle for lake trout. Line anchors and trolling weights along with a Heddon saltwater rod and reel are pictured here. Other wheel house fixtures include a hand-carved net float, a torpedo used to measure distance when dragged behind the boat, a handmade housing for a floating compass illuminated by a small kerosene lamp, and, on the far right-hand side of the wheel house, a kerosene signal lamp. From the collection of Ron Adamson.

Perfection, Restigouche, Peerless, Griswold, Cascapedia, Tobique, and Colonel Thompson, are highly prized collectibles today, as are the countless custom reels vom Hofe produced during his career. But although he built many types of reels, including baitcasting and trolling reels for both fresh water and salt water, his fly reels remain the most cherished models among collectors.

The reel makers of the mid- to late-1800s built many exceptional reels. When an angler bought one of these reels, he took home a finely tuned piece of machinery. However, even the best reels demanded oiling or required occasional repair. Usually, an angler needed to disassemble the reel to oil or repair it—a process that required considerable time and effort. It was a headache to take out a series of screws, take off the end plate and spool, oil the moving parts, and then line everything up and put the screws back in, especially if an angler had to disassemble the reel while on a lake or stream. To make their reels more user-friendly, builders began experimenting with quick-takedown features, which allowed anglers to take their reels apart easily.

Charles W. MacCord of Weehawken, New Jersey, received the first patent for a quick-takedown multiplying reel in 1874. Other reel makers patented their own quick-takedown designs in the decades that followed. The first commercial reel with the feature was Julius vom Hofe's President model, patented in 1892, which allowed for easy removal of the spool. By the early 1900s, quick-takedown designs became more common, but not every reel manufacturer adapted the design to its reels.

A New Century

While reel makers like Edward and Julius vom Hofe were building top-of-the-line, handmade reels for anglers who wanted nothing but the best, other companies aimed for the average angler, mass producing reliable but affordable reels.

One of the most notable reel producers was August F. Meisselbach of Newark, New Jersey, who built durable, quality reels the average angler could afford. In 1885, at the age of twenty, Meisselbach received his first patent for a single-action reel called the Amateur. In 1888, Meisselbach, who went into business with his brother William, came out with another single-action reel called the Expert. Both reels sold well and helped push A. F. Meisselbach & Brother into the arena as a respected reel builder. The brothers' Allright and Featherlight fly reels appeared in the late 1890s and experienced tremendous success. As the new century arrived, A. F. Meisselbach had earned a place among the top reel builders in the country and even experienced brisk sales in Europe. In the first decade of the 1900s, the Take-Apart and Tripart takedown models fueled the company's success and helped set a standard for takedown reels. Until 1917, when the brothers sold their company, A. F. Meisselbach produced a long list of memorable reels that collectors treasure today. The Meisselbach reels continued in pro-

duction until 1941 through the Otto Heineman Phonograph Supply Co. of New York City, which later became General Industries. Heineman sold the reels under the name A. F. Meisselbach Manufacturing Company, but few of those reels matched the quality of the reels produced by August and William.

The late 1910s and early 1920s saw a dramatic increase in the number of companies that manufactured fishing reels, and competition began to rise. Among those companies was the Meisselbach-Catucci Corporation of Newark, New Jersey. A. F. Meisselbach started the business with Pliny Catucci as a gear manufacturer in conjunction with A. F. Meisselbach & Brother. It was not until 1921, well after August and William sold their company, that Catucci began manufacturing reels with A. F. Meisselbach employees. The company produced such models as the Symplopart and Brakelite and became one of the top reel companies in the United States during the 1920s. After the business was sold to the Bronson Reel Company of Bronson, Michigan, in 1931, the Meisselbach-Catucci models were eventually discontinued when Bronson was forced to trim production due to the economic pressures of the Great Depression.

Big-Game Saltwater Reels

The 1910s also witnessed a popularity surge in big-game, saltwater reels. Fishing in Florida and California for monster, ocean-dwelling species such as the tarpon and tuna started to catch on in the 1890s. A few reel manufacturers, like Julius vom Hofe, tried to fill the void in big-game reels by developing strong, reliable reels that could handle the stresses of extremely large fish and the abuse of salt water.

Although the early big-game reels were built well, they had one major problem. When an enormous fish like a tarpon took a bait and ran, it stripped line off the reel at a terrifying rate. While the spool was spinning out of control, so was the crank handle. If an angler tried to grab the handle while it was spinning, he was in danger of injuring his hand or fingers. William Boschen of New York came up with a solution to the problem by designing a drag-and-clutch system for big-game reels. The anti-reverse mechanism he developed kept the handle still while the spool was spinning. His design went into production through Julius vom Hofe. Although it was not an instant success, Boschen's reel eventually gained acceptance in 1913, when he used it to catch the first broad-billed swordfish with a rod and reel. Boschen's fish, which was caught off of California's Catalina Island, weighed 358 pounds (163 kg).

Other reel manufacturers began producing their own lines of off-shore reels, and by the 1920s, reel builders such as Joseph A. Coxe of Los Angeles, California, and the Bronson Reel Company were

PFLUEGER **TEMPLAR** REEL

Pflueger Templar Reel

Saltwater anglers who wanted to buy a Pflueger reel during the 1920s could purchase the company's Templar model. The reel featured a patented handle drag, a drag stop, leather thumb brake, and an easy oiling system. Pflueger claimed the reel could withstand the terrific strains of all saltwater fishing. This illustration appeared in a 1928 Pflueger catalog, which offered seven versions of the Templar, ranging in price from thirty to sixty dollars.

Largest
MARLIN
SWORDFISH

ever taken in the
Atlantic Ocean
with Rod
and Reel

Weight . . 502 pounds
Length . 12 feet, 2 inches
Time of Landing . 6 hours
Taken off CAT CAY in
the BAHAMAS, by
Mrs. Anne Moore,
New York City,
March, 1933

Tackle used:
PFLUEGER ATLAPAC
9/0 REEL
PFLUEGER TARPSAIL LINE
PFLUEGER SOBEY HOOK

Above: **Largest marlin**

An angler testimonial like this one, which appeared on the back cover of a 1938 Pflueger catalog, made a major impact on consumers. Nothing could endorse Pflueger's saltwater reel better than the largest marlin ever caught in the Atlantic Ocean with a rod and reel.

Left: **Edward vom Hofe salmon reel**

Edward vom Hofe & Company of New York City made some of the finest reels any angler has ever had the pleasure to use. This salmon reel, from the collection of Andy Foster, was produced in 1882.

building popular, high-quality models. The 1930s marked a change in big-game reel design. Most early off-shore trolling reels were complex pieces of engineering that were difficult to maintain, but in the 1930s, that trend changed as reel manufacturers simplified designs to make their reels more user friendly.

One of the big-game personalities who helped push off-shore angling into the international spotlight was author Zane Grey. His adventures of battling the world's largest fish were recorded in his numerous books, such as *Tales of Swordfish and Tuna* and *Tales of Fishing Virgin Seas*. His adventures were legendary and encouraged other anglers to pursue the sport. Grey was so renowned for his angling accomplishments that Hardy Brothers of Alnwick, England, paid tribute to him by building a line of Zane Grey reels in the 1930s.

Saltwater as well as freshwater reels received a boost in 1916 with the introduction of stainless steel. Although stainless steel was not a perfect material, it resisted pitting better than steel and found its way into reel design, especially in saltwater reels. Twentieth-century technology made another leap in 1926, when the process of anodizing aluminum opened the door for the widespread use of aluminum alloys in reel building. Of course, reel makers experimented with aluminum during the 1800s and early 1900s, but the protective oxide coating provided by the anodizing process made it much more practical to use aluminum alloys in reel design. The result was a new breed of reels that were lighter and resisted the elements better than reels built from more traditional metals. Although anodized aluminum was light and durable, plastic was just as light and would never rust. It made its debut in the tackle industry in the 1920s and eventually found a permanent home in reel design.

The Spinning Reel

One of the great innovations in reel design during the first half of the twentieth century was the introduction of the spinning reel. The spinning reel marked a dramatic change in reel design from the traditional multipliers and single-action reels that dominated the tackle industry during the 1800s and early 1900s. The idea behind its design was to eliminate the backlash and spool overrun common to winch-type reels. The spinning reel's spool sits perpendicular to the rod, as opposed to the winch-type reel, which has a spool that moves in the same direction as the rod. The difference is that line tends to fall off the spool of the spinning reel during the cast and does not overrun. In contrast, line pulls the spool of the winch-type reel so the spool can continue to spin when the line hits the water, resulting in overrun and tangles.

In the last decades of the 1800s, a few reel makers, like Peter Malloch of Scotland, experimented with designs conceptually resembling the spinning reel. However, during the first decades of the twentieth century, Alfred Holden Illingworth of England developed the design that today's anglers are familiar with. Illingworth's first Thread Line Spinning Reel incorporated a moving spool and a stationary bail. He refined the design, however, and in later models the spool remained stationary, while the bail revolved as it does on today's spinning reels. Although Illingworth's invention eventually took reel making in a whole new direction, his Thread Line Spinning Reel did not receive universal acclaim. It was not until the years following World War II that the spinning reel's popularity exploded in the United States. Its rise in popularity was partly due to the introduction of monofilament line, which was a light and efficient partner to the spinning reel. However, most of the ever-increasing number of anglers in America gravitated toward the spinning reel because they could cast easily and accurately with it.

When the popularity of the spinning reel did take off, some reel makers stuck with Illingworth's open-spool design, while others experimented with a closed-spool spinning reel in the 1950s and 1960s. The closed-spool design used a revolving-toothed wheel instead of the metal bail to collect line on the spool. A small hole in the front cover helped guide the line, and a push button at the rear of the reel released the wheel to cast. The closed-cover spinning reels were even easier to use than the open spinning reels, because an angler did not have to flip the bail and hold the loose line with a finger when casting. A simple push of a button did all the work. Although the closed-spool reel experienced a few decades of popularity and remains in production (especially in children's reels), its following has faded. Improvements in bail design of the open-spool spinning reel have made it just as easy to use, and today it is the most popular design.

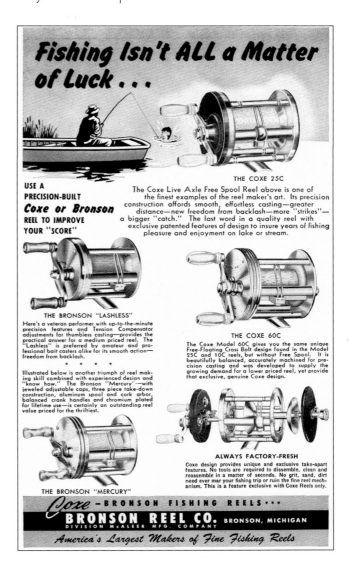

Coxe-Bronson reels

Fishing isn't all a matter of luck, as this 1948 advertisement for Coxe and Bronson reels suggests. Investing in a reel that carried a reputable name like Coxe or Bronson could indeed improve an angler's score.

Through the last 150 years of the fishing reel's development, hundreds of companies and individual reel makers have contributed innovations and ideas, producing a rich web of reels that collectors pursue today. Companies such as Pflueger; Shakespeare; Heddon; South Bend; the Andrew B. Hendryx Company of New Haven, Connecticut; the Martin Automatic Fishing Reel Company of Mohawk, New York; the William H. Talbot Reel and Manufacturing Company of Kansas City, Missouri; and others each carved out a place in the evolution of the reel and set the standard for the reel makers who followed. Today their work lives on in the hearts of collectors who cherish the wonderful reels they produced.

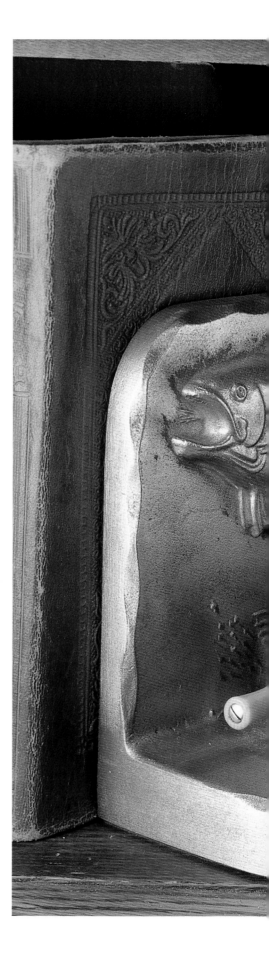

Above: **Pflueger fun**

Fishing advertising does not always have to use eye-popping testimonials or action-packed sensationalism to be effective. In this 1937 advertisement, Pflueger takes a shot at using a bit of tongue-in-cheek humor to sell its reels and lures.

Right: **The classics**

Like the artists who wrote these classic books, the classic reels pictured here were the products of craftspeople who invested hours of time and care in their craft—reels built with as much care as the crafting of fine watches. Memorabilia owner: Andy Foster.

Chapter 3

Lures

Main photo: **Patience**

Although opening day may be months away, it's never too early to clean and oil your tackle for the coming season. Memorabilia owner: Pete Press.

Inset: **1929 Abbey & Imbrie catalog**

Abbey & Imbrie was one of many retailers that sold fishing tackle through catalogs. In contrast to catalogs issued by individual tackle manufacturers, retail catalogs offered rods, reels and lures produced by a variety of companies. During the 1920s, Abbey & Imbrie was one of the oldest and most well-established tackle retailers in North America.

Through the course of angling's evolution, lure builders and buyers have struggled to find the ultimate lure. There is no lure that is perfectly suited for all times and places, however. For a fly fisherman or -woman, the ideal lure could be a No. 10 Muddler Minnow one day and a No. 18 Quill Gordon the next. For a bass angler, it may be a Jitterbug in the morning and a black, rubber worm in the afternoon. Factors such as the season, time of day, amount of light, water and air temperature, strength of wind, approaching fronts, and water clarity create so many variables in fishing that anglers commonly carry a vast array of lures to cover all their needs. When they are not on the water, anglers continually search for better lures to add to their assortment. At the other end of the angling market, lure builders continue to churn out new products to meet the demand. Some are innovative or revolutionary, others just variations of time-honored ideas.

In the wake of more than 150 years of commercial lure sales lies a rich collage of thousands upon thousands of brands and styles that have come and gone over the decades. Collectors sort through the seemingly endless line of artificial baits, mainly those produced from the late 1800s to the mid-1900s, trying to find the lure of a lifetime or to add another interesting piece to their collection.

Origins of the Lure

It is difficult to pinpoint what primitive culture first used artificial lures. Hooks carved from bone, shell, wood, and stone were the first forms of lures, but no one is certain where the hook originated. Archaeologists have unearthed primitive hooks created thousands of years ago by Native American tribes. Archaeologists know that Eskimos, Inuits, and other Native Americans living in the northern half of the continent used ice-spearing decoys more than three thousand years ago, and evidence suggests that some of their tribes also attached hooks to their decoys.

In *Da Natura Animallum*, Claudius Aelian, a Roman writer who lived from 230–170 B.C., described Macedonian anglers who attached feathers to hooks to catch fish. Historians believe this is the oldest written reference to fly fishing, but the practice of angling with flies probably began long before that. There is also evidence in the form of hieroglyphics, which suggests that ancient Egyptians may have connected feathers to hooks.

Hand-painted Phantom Minnows

These are colorful examples of the lure that retained the same basic form from 1800–1940.

Although the very early evolution of lures remains a bit sketchy, the findings prove that the practice of using artificial baits is not a modern innovation.

In Europe, anglers began making metal fishing hooks during the Bronze and Iron Ages. During the Middle Ages, anglers started fashioning hooks from steel. Historians believe anglers started fly fishing in Europe somewhere around the twelfth century, but there is no solid evidence pointing to the first use of flies on the continent. The evolutionary path of the lure starts to gain clarity during the 1400s. Dame Juliana Berners's *Treatyse of Fysshynge wyth an Angle*, published in London in 1496, describes specific fly patterns used to match hatches of insects. She also mentions a metal bait resembling a fish that flashed erratically in the water. Her writing suggests that the use of artificial baits was well established by the fifteenth century.

By the time Izaak Walton published *The Compleat Angler* in 1653, fly fishing was a prolific sport in Great Britain. Walton's descriptions of fly fishing helped to promote the sport and popularize the idea of using artificial baits to catch trout and salmon. Flies remained the predominant artificial bait until the 1800s, but anglers

Rare classics

The lures on display here are considered extremely rare. They were made by Ray Thompson (1887–1966) of Park Rapids, Minnesota. Ray was known as somewhat of a scoundrel moonshiner and poacher, making him probably as colorful as his decoys and lures—most of which were whittled while Ray was behind bars. Memorabilia owner: Carter Stenberg.

began experimenting with various forms of metal baits resembling spoons or spinners before that time.

Commercial Lures

The scope of artificial lures started to change in the first decade of the nineteenth century with the introduction of the False or Phantom Minnow, the predecessor of the modern plug. Although it was the first mass-produced lure, the Phantom Minnow was probably not the first commercial artificial bait. It appeared around the turn of the century in Britain and made its way to North America by 1810.

As its name suggests, the Phantom Minnow resembled a baitfish. It had a metal head, a torpedo-shaped body made from silk, and metal spinner fins that sat on either side of its head. Evenly spaced along the body were two or three sets of double or treble hooks. A pattern of scales and dots ornamented the body. One of bait's innovative features was the use of both barbed and treble hooks, which remains a standard in plug manufacturing today. Amazingly enough, the Phantom Minnow continued in production until the 1940s. Manufacturers modified the design over time, but the basic form remained the same for nearly 150 years. Manufacturers began offering models with a rubber coating over the silk in the late 1800s and also

Above: **Phantom Minnow**
This classic bait style was the first lure to be mass produced.

Left: **Victorian fishing**
These century-old baits and tackle are fine examples of the distinctive craftsmanship and design of the romantic Victorian era. The prize lure in this photograph, located in the handmade wood-and-leather tackle box's cover, is the American Spinner made by John B. McHarg. Among the other lures and fishing equipment shown here in their original packaging is the Adirondack Spinner. Memorabilia owner: Arlen Carter.

added various colors and sizes to their selection through the years. In the 1900s, manufacturers introduced a wooden version known as the Ideal Phantom.

Because rod and reel technology did not allow for effective

baitcasting in the early decades of the nineteenth century, the Phantom Minnow's arrival on the fishing scene did not set off an explosion in the commercial lure market. As the builders of rods and reels created better baitcasting equipment in the latter half of the 1800s, the lure industry started to take off.

Julio Thompson Buel of Whitehall, New York, received the first United States patent for an artificial lure in 1852 with his Arrowhead Spinner. A few years prior to developing his spinner bait, Buel had invented and started commercially producing fishing spoons from his shop in Whitehall. Whether fact or fiction, the legend of how he invented the spoon has been handed down through the years from one generation of anglers to the next. According to the story, Buel was fishing on Vermont's Lake Bomoseen. He caught his share of fish during the morning and decided to settle down for lunch, but as he was preparing to eat, his drifting boat struck a rock. The jolt from the impact caused his spoon to fall from his lunch bucket into the water. Buel helplessly watched his spoon sink toward the bottom, when suddenly a fish darted from the shadows and devoured the shiny eating utensil. A revelation hit the young angler, and soon after he began experimenting with spoon baits. At first, Buel used the discovery to make baits for his own use, but after moving to Whitehall, he started his own business in 1848 called the J. T. Buel Company.

Spoons gave Buel his first taste of commercial success, and it was only four years after he started manufacturing them that he received the patent for his Arrowhead Spinner. The Spinner was not originally available as a complete lure. During its early production, Buel sold only the arrow-shaped spinner portion of the bait. Anglers needed to build a wire framework for the spinner and attach their own hook. Later, Buel added a frame and a single treble hook to the bait. The Arrowhead Spinner remained in production for more than eighty years, so it is a relatively common collectible to run across.

Despite Buel's contributions to the development of both the spoon and spinner, his baits remain somewhat of a footnote in angling history. His work became overshadowed by the popular plug makers of the late 1800s and early 1900s. Regardless, Buel was a major force in the lure industry. He produced thousands of artificial baits over a span of almost forty years, manufacturing a wide variety of spoons and spinners for both casting and trolling that were sold to anglers all across the country.

Not long after Buel received his first patent, a Painesville, Ohio, gunsmith named Riley Haskell patented what went on to become the most valuable lure ever made, the Haskell Trolling Bait, commonly referred to today as the Haskell Minnow. In the late 1980s, one of the few surviving examples of Haskell's lure sold for just over $20,000, which was the highest price ever paid for a fishing collectible at that time. In the years since, collectors have paid considerably more for antique tackle, but it was Haskell's Minnow that set off the first notable price explosion in the fishing collectibles market.

Gems of wood

This old wooden tackle box holds an early Heddon Dummy Double and a striped Charmer by the Charmer Minnow Company of Springfield, Missouri. Memorabilia owner: Pete Press.

Like the Phantom Minnow before it, the Haskell Minnow looked like a small fish. It differed from the Phantom in that it more strongly resembled a minnow—it had eyes, gills, a mouth, fins, and, in some cases, scales, although Haskell commonly placed the markings on only one side of the unpainted, metal bait. Haskell produced the lure in three sizes, ranging in body length from three and one-half to six inches (9–15 cm). Each had the distinct, streamlined shape of a fish and was equipped with just one double hook, connected to the rotating tail section. The Haskell Minnow's 1859 patent called for the use of wood as a potential material for its construction, but it is doubtful Haskell ever produced any wooden models during its more than fifteen years of production. If he did, collectors have yet to find one. Collectors have unearthed more than three dozen Haskell Minnows, but all of them are copper, brass, or a combination of the two.

Metal artificial baits remained the norm in the commercial industry until the turn of the century. However, lure manufacturers began integrating wood into the design of their baits in the 1870s. Charles Dunbar and David Huard of Ashland, Wisconsin, received the first patent for a wooden-bodied artificial lure in 1874, but H. C. Brush of Brushes Mills, New York, was the first to manufacture a lure built with wood. To say Brush's Floating Spinner, patented in 1876, was a wooden bait, however, would be misleading. His bait consisted of a metal spinner equipped with a cork body and a treble hook.

In 1883, Harry Comstock of Fulton, New York, patented a wooden-bodied bait called the Flying Helgramite. This bizarre-looking bait featured two large, awkward metal spinners connected to the sides of a turned wooden body. A double hook hung off the end of each winglike spinner, and a treble hook dangled from a loop connected to the metal tail piece. Raised, glass eyes sat on either side of its rounded head. Comstock sold his lure to Ernest F. Pflueger's Enterprise Manufacturing Company of Akron, Ohio, that same year. Pflueger modified the bait by coating it with his innovative luminous paint, also patented in 1883. The Flying Helgramite came in four different sizes, ranging in price from 80¢ to $1.25. Advertisements claimed that the bait would not sink or snag and was "exactly like life." Although a sight to behold, the Flying Helgramite did not last long in production. A little more than a year later, Pflueger stopped manufacturing the bait—quite possibly because it scared more fish than it caught. The short life span of the Flying Helgramite makes it a rare and valuable collectible today.

Heddon Luny Frog

Heddon's popular Luny Frog was first introduced in 1927. Because it was made from pyralin, it marked a departure from wooden-plug production and became one of the first successful plastic lures on the market.

Heddon

A beekeeper from Dowagiac, Michigan, named James Heddon changed the course of lure making during the 1890s. Collectors credit Heddon more than any one individual with having the greatest effect on the artificial lure industry. Heddon invented the plug, or wooden lure, and started an avalanche of plug development. The now-famous legend of how Heddon stumbled upon the idea for a wooden bait has many variable details, but the basic story describes him sitting by the waterside of the mill pond at Dowagiac Creek whittling a piece of wood while he waited for a friend. After carving for a while, Heddon threw the piece of wood out over the water, and a bass went after it. The idea took root and the plug was born.

Historians speculate that Heddon started carving wooden baits somewhere between 1890 and 1892, although the exact year is up for debate. Heddon's family had carved wooden ice decoys since the 1850s, so he was familiar with the tradition of carving wooden shapes as lures for fish—he just added hooks to his carvings so anglers could cast or troll them with a rod and reel. Collectors believe the first carved bait Heddon worked on was a frog, equipped with a treble hook hanging from the belly and single hooks connected to each leg.

Cracklebacks

This Heddon collection includes the Underwater Minnow, Near-Surface Wiggler, Crab Wiggler, and Artistic Minnow. The Heddon rod is a split-bamboo Musky Special and the reel is a 3-35 model. Memorabilia owner: Carter Stenberg.

Above: "Want Fish?"

The popularity of Heddon baits was not limited to the company's selection of plugs. Other baits such as the "HEP" Spinner also made their mark on the tackle industry.

Left: Heddon plugs

This colorful collection of lures, rod, and reel hails from one of the most famous plug manufacturers of the twentieth century, James Heddon & Sons of Dowagiac, Michigan. On the line here is a rare frogskin-patterned, propped Spin-Diver, made from 1918 to 1926. From the collection of Arlen Carter.

Just after the turn of the century, Heddon started his tackle company, working out of his house in the beginning. In 1902 he received the first patent for his slope-nose Fish-Bait, which customers later knew as the Dowagiac Perfect Surface Casting Bait, Dowagiac Expert, and the "200." Sons William and Charles joined the business in 1903 and 1904 respectively. Together the trio launched James Heddon & Sons into the forefront of the artificial bait industry. They worked hard to promote their baits as the ultimate fishing lures. During the first decade of production, lures such as the Dowagiac Underwater Expert, Dowagiac Minnow, Surface Minnow, Killer, Artistic Minnow, Dowagiac Muskollonge Minnow, and Swimming Minnow helped establish the company name. By 1910, anglers all over the United States and Canada were familiar with Heddon baits. In the decades that followed, the company continued to expand, producing a long list of memorable lures, including the Crab Wiggler, Lucky 13, Vampire, Luny Frog, Spin-Diver, Saltwater Special, Crazy Crawler, and River Runt. The business grew from selling less than ten thousand lures a year in 1902, to producing more than ten thousand baits per day in 1950.

James Heddon died in 1911, but his sons stayed with the company, renaming it James Heddon's Sons. Charles remained in Dowagiac and ran the company until his death in 1941. William moved to Florida and worked on the research and development end of the business until he died a few years after his brother. The company remained in family hands until 1955, when Heddon's grandson John sold it to an outside buyer in Texas. The company tumbled downward after the sale and lost much of the respect the Heddons had worked so hard to build. Today, Pradco Incorporated of Fort Smith, Arkansas, owns the rights to the name and still manufactures a few of the lures.

The Heddon company captured the attention of collectors because it produced a large number of high-quality lures over a long period of time. Heddon & Sons strove to remain in the forefront of lure development. Whenever an innovation in lure design hit the market, it seemed Heddon & Sons was there to lead the way.

Pflueger

Long before James Heddon carved his first plug, Ernest F. Pflueger started his own tackle company in Akron, Ohio. Pflueger's product advertisements claim the first year of business as 1864, but that is a bit misleading. Pflueger started his tackle business, called the Enterprise Manufacturing Company, in 1881. Around the same time, he bought the American Fish Hook Company of Akron, which was founded in 1864. In an attempt to add credibility to his business, Pflueger began using 1864 as the year his company was founded.

Illuminating lures

Luminous baits were a long-running standard in Pflueger catalogs, first appearing in the early 1880s when Ernest F. Pflueger founded the company and patented his luminous paint. In order to achieve the optimal luminous effect when fishing at night, it was recommended that anglers expose the lure to natural or artificial light for the same amount of time they would be fishing. Among the luminous versions of plugs listed in this 1928 catalog were the Surprise and Neverfail Minnows, and the Wizard Wiggler.

Pflueger plugs

Less than five years after this 1928 Pflueger catalog was issued, the company made the decision to significantly cut back on its lure production and focus its energy on building reels. Pre-1930 versions of lures such as the Kent Frog, Magnet, and Neverfail are among the most highly regarded Pflueger collectibles.

Pflueger fishing tackle catalog, 1928

Until the turn of the century, Pflueger manufactured a variety of baits ranging from metal spinners to flies, while establishing a reputation for quality fishing tackle.

The first documented lures produced by Pflueger were the fish-shaped Dexter Spoon and a glass-bodied, luminous spinner called the Crystal Minnow. It is not certain exactly what year the lures first appeared, but surviving catalogs verify their production in the early 1880s. In the years leading up to 1900, Pflueger manufactured a variety of lures, including the Success Spinner, Florida Bass Bait, Pearl Phantom, Moskollonge Minnow, and the notorious Flying

Pflueger Pal-O-Mine Minnow

The Pal-O-Mine was one of the most popular and effective plugs produced by Pflueger. These illustrations of the bait appeared in the company's 1928 catalog.

"Baits that Catch Fish"

This 1924 Shakespeare catalog ad shows some of the lures that helped establish the company as one of the top tackle manufacturers in North America; it includes the Slim Jim, Mouse, and Pikie Kazoo.

Helgramite, which was produced in 1883 and wore a coat of Pflueger's newly patented luminous paint. Pflueger used materials such as metal, rubber, pearl, and glass in the construction of his early baits.

Not long before James Heddon patented his Fish-Bait, Pflueger began producing his own wooden baits. One of Pflueger's earliest plugs, the Trory Minnow, first appeared around the turn of the century. The plugs were equipped with treble hooks and propeller blades. The bait is an extremely rare find today. A few years later, the company introduced the Wizard Minnow, followed by more diverse offerings that included a series of Monarch Minnows and the Kent Frog, as well as other popular models like the Globe, Neverfail Minnow, Surprise Minnow, and the Pal-O-Mine.

Pflueger's Enterprise Manufacturing Company remained a major force in the lure industry until the 1930s, when it decided to direct its attention toward manufacturing reels. The company did not stop lure production altogether, but significantly trimmed it. In 1965, the company changed its name to the Pflueger Corporation, and one year later, the Shakespeare Company bought Pflueger.

Shakespeare

William Shakespeare Jr. of Kalamazoo, Michigan, entered the commercial tackle market as a reel maker in the mid-1890s. By 1900, he had issued his first lure, the wooden-bodied Revolution. As the name implies, Shakespeare's bait was revolutionary, because it introduced free-spinning propeller blades to the fishing world. The tubular wooden bait was built with two sections and three sets of treble hooks, one on each side and one behind. The propellers were placed in the front, back, or middle of the bait. On one version, Shakespeare attempted to prevent line twist by using a pair of propellers that moved in opposite directions. Advertisements claimed that Shakespeare sold 1,200 of the innovative lures in the first year of production. In 1901, he received his first patent for the wooden-bodied version of the Revolution, but by then Shakespeare had already begun using aluminum instead of wood in its construction. He applied for a patent on the aluminum model the same year.

In the first decade of the twentieth century, the William Shakespeare Jr. Company gained a foothold in the lure industry with such lures as the Evolution, Wooden Minnow, Slim Jim, and Punkin-Seed. In the decades that followed, Shakespeare produced a wide variety of baits, along with rods, reels, and other tackle, and became one of America's prominent tackle companies. Following William Shakespeare Jr.'s death in 1952, the Creek Chub Bait Company of Garrett, Indiana, bought the business.

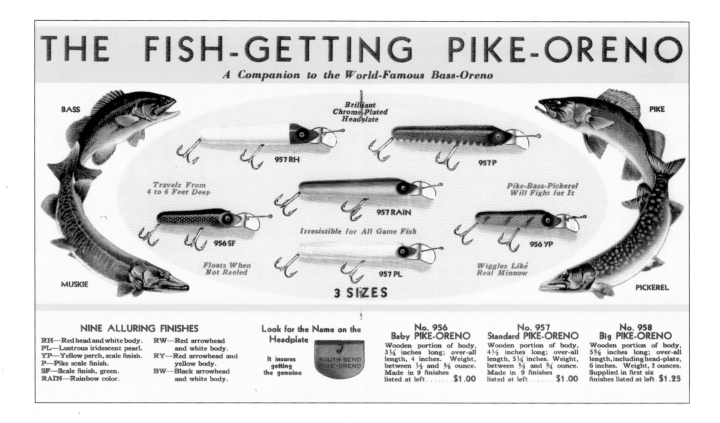

South Bend

Another important invention in lure design to emerge in the last decade of the nineteenth century was the bucktail bait, which was a lure with deer hair attached at the rear to help cover the hooks and provide additional action. F. G. Worden of South Bend, Indiana, invented the bucktail and began producing it in the mid-1890s. The bait's popularity soared around the turn of the century, and Worden worked out a deal that allowed Shakespeare to build a wooden version of the bait called the Shakespeare-Worden Bucktail Spinner. At the same time, Worden sold his own bucktail baits through his Worden Bucktail Bait Company.

In 1909, the company was acquired by F. A. Bryan, F. L. Denis, and B. W. Oliver, also of South Bend, Indiana, who changed its name to the South Bend Bait Company. During the decade that followed, South Bend introduced an extensive list of baits, which included the Underwater Minnow, Combination Minnow, Min-Buck Minnow, Muskie Trolling and Muskie Casting Minnows, Bass-Oreno, and Surf-Oreno. By World War I, South Bend had grown to become one of the top tackle manufacturers in North America, and even grabbed a market share in Europe. South Bend remained a major tackle manufacturer until 1965, when it was purchased by B. F. Gladding & Co. of Syracuse, New York. South Bend lost much of its prominence in the 1970s, but new management started a comeback in the 1980s, and the company eventually regained its place among the top tackle producers in the country.

Pike-Oreno

Color pages like this one from a 1932 South Bend catalog help collectors identify the various versions of a lure produced during a specific year. This advertisement reveals that there were three different sizes of the Pike-Oreno issued in 1932, and it was available in nine different finishes.

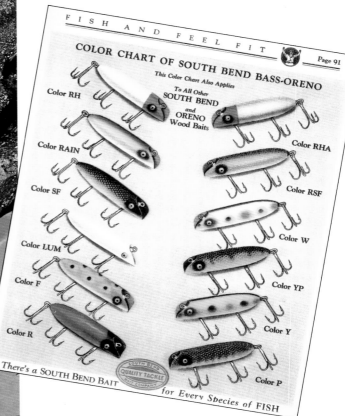

Above: **Bass-Oreno**

The Bass-Oreno was the flagship of South Bend baits. No other lure produced by the company was as popular or recognizable. This 1929 catalog color chart illustrates a dozen different versions of the bait.

Left: **Floaters**

Surface lures prove to be very annoying to the territorial bass. This collection includes South Bend's Bass-Oreno, Two-Oreno, and Baby Surface Oreno, as well as Pflueger's Surprise Minnow and Magic Minnow. Owner: Pete Press.

The ones that got away

Watch out for low-hanging wires! This aerial snag is filled with classic tackle from the collection of Pete Press.

Creek Chub

The Creek Chub Bait Company of Garrett, Indiana, started in 1916 as three men and one lure. Henry Dills, Carl Heinzerling, and George Schluthesis joined forces to manufacture their Creek Chub Wiggler, a wooden plug they named after a familiar baitfish. The company's first commercial lure was the No. 100 Wiggler. Soon after its introduction, Creek Chub came out with its second type of lure called the Crawdad, which eventually became one of the company's most popular lures.

In 1919, Creek Chub introduced its most famous lure, the Pikie Minnow, which it manufactured in numerous variations through the years. The Pikie Minnow, with its wooden body, metal lip, and sloped nose, proved popular, because it worked extremely well on northerns, muskies, and bass. Other Creek Chub models such as the Darter and Husky Musky appeared during the 1920s.

One of Creek Chub's most significant contributions to the lure industry was the natural-scale finish it developed for plugs. Dills invented the finish, and Creek Chub received a patent for it in 1918. The natural-scale effect was achieved by placing mesh in front of the lure and spray-painting through it, leaving a pattern of scales on the body. It became such a successful innovation that other manufacturers paid Creek Chub to use the technique.

The Creek Chub Bait Company was run by the descendants of its founders until 1978, when Carl Heinzerling's son, Harry Heinzerling, sold the business to the Lazy Ike Company of Fort Dodge, Iowa.

Flip-Flap

Among Creek Chub's diverse offering of lures during the 1930s was the Flip-Flap, which is shown here in the company's 1935 catalog.

"The Pikie"

For decades, Creek Chub's Pikie lures were among the most effective baits on the market. The company slogan claimed "Creek Chub Baits Catch More Fish," and that was certainly true of the Pikie. Today, Pikie lures are highly sought-after collectibles.

World-class lure

Creek Chub's Pikie Minnow was so popular, many companies tried to copy its design. Collectors often run across examples of its numerous imitations, but a real Pikie can be identified by the "C.C.B. Co." stamped on the mouthpiece.

1942 Creek Chub catalog cover

Husky Musky

When most collectors think of Creek Chub, the first lure that comes to mind is the Pikie, but the company manufactured many memorable lures over the years, including the Husky Musky.

Creek Chub Wiggler

This illustration of the Creek Chub Wiggler appeared in the company's 1935 catalog.

Moonlight/Paw Paw

Nearly a decade before the Creek Chub Bait Company was founded, Horace Ball and Charles Varney started a lure business called the Moonlight Bait Company. Ball took the name from a fishing club that he and his friends in Paw Paw, Michigan, had formed. The club members worked during the day and fished together at night. Ball started carving wooden baits for the outings, and his lures proved to be effective.

In 1908, Ball and Varney formed the company and began producing their first lure, the Moonlight Floating Bait. The lure was a rather plain-looking plug with three treble hooks. The pair swore the coating of luminous paint they applied to the bait made it more visible and therefore more effective for night fishing. Ads proclaimed the bait "self-glowing and attractive" and said, "Use the Moonlight Bait on a moonlight or a dark night, and your fine string of fish will make you a convert and surprise your neighbor."

During the early years of the business, Ball and Varney assembled their lures in the basement of Paw Paw city hall. The company grew quickly and gained a share of the national market. Ball and Varney introduced other baits including the Trout Bob, Fish

Paw Paw

According to the Michigan company, each lifelike frog lure produced by Paw Paw "Sits like a frog, Kicks like a frog, Looks like a frog." This collection of memorabilia is owned by Jerry Grayling.

Nipple-rubber, Underwater Minnow, Dreadnought, and Pearl Wobbler.

In 1923, the Moonlight Bait Company merged with the Novelty Works of Dowagiac, Michigan, to become the Moonlight Bait and Novelty Works. In 1927, the Paw Paw Bait Company purchased Moonlight, but it remained a separate business until Paw Paw incorporated it in 1935. The Paw Paw Bait Company remained in business until 1970, when it was purchased by Shakespeare.

The wooden plugs produced by these and other commercial manufacturers during the first few decades of the twentieth century are the lures collectors cherish most. Of course, other memorable lures appeared in the first half of the twentieth century. The Fred Arbogast Company of Akron, Ohio, introduced its floating bass bait called the Jitterbug in 1937, and one year later, the Kautzky Manufacturing Company of Fort Dodge, Iowa, patented the Lazy Ike, invented by Newell Daniels of Fort Dodge.

The wooden plugs manu-factured during the 1930s marked the end of an era. Wooden plugs had dominated the lure-building industry for nearly a half century, but technological advancements were pushing wood out of the market. During the 1920s, plastic started replacing wood as a plug material. The Vesco Bait Company of New York City, New York, produced the first plastic plugs in 1922, and other companies gradually followed suit. Plastic plugs were cheaper to produce and

Frogs

Light rain, lily pads, and fallen logs make the bass fisherman's or -woman's blood pressure rise. This collection of frogs includes Paw Paw's Wotta-Frog, Jenson's wooden Froglegs, Heddon's Luny Frog, Hastings's Weedless Rubber Frog, the All Star Bait Company's Gee-Wiz Frog, and a Christensen Frog. Memorabilia owner: Pete Press.

Above: **Daredevil meets Dardevle**

This fish is truly a risk-taker as he boldly chases Lou Eppinger's irresistible Dardevle lure. Eppinger created the bait's unusual spelling to appease churchgoers who thought that a "devil" had no place in their tackle boxes.

Right: **The Dardevle**

In 1906, Lou J. Eppinger of Detroit, Michigan, introduced a painted spoon to the fishing world, which he named the Osprey. He later renamed the bait the Dardevle, and it went on to become one of the most popular fishing lures ever created. Though tackle manufacturers like J. T. Buel were selling spoons decades before the introduction of the Dardevle, Eppinger's idea of painting the spoon proved to be a revolutionary advancement in lure design.

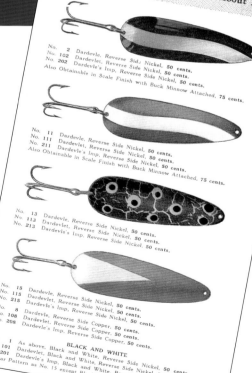

Dardevle Changed a Nation's Ideas About Fishing

No. 2 Dardevle, Reverse Side Nickel, 50 cents.
No. 102 Dardevlet, Reverse Side Nickel, 50 cents.
No. 202 Dardevle's Imp. Reverse Side Nickel, 50 cents.
Also Obtainable in Scale Finish with Buck Minnow Attached, 75 cents.

No. 11 Dardevle, Reverse Side Nickel, 50 cents.
No. 111 Dardevlet, Reverse Side Nickel, 50 cents.
No. 211 Dardevle's Imp. Reverse Side Nickel, 50 cents.
Also Obtainable in Scale Finish with Buck Minnow Attached, 75 cents.

No. 13 Dardevle, Reverse Side Nickel, 50 cents.
No. 113 Dardevlet, Reverse Side Nickel, 50 cents.
No. 213 Dardevle's Imp. Reverse Side Nickel, 50 cents.

No. 15 Dardevle, Reverse Side Nickel, 50 cents.
No. 115 Dardevlet, Reverse Side Nickel, 50 cents.
No. 215 Dardevle's Imp. Reverse Side Nickel, 50 cents.
No. 8 Dardevle, Reverse Side Copper, 50 cents.
No. 108 Dardevlet, Reverse Side Copper, 50 cents.
No. 208 Dardevle's Imp. Reverse Side Copper, 50 cents.

BLACK AND WHITE
No. 1 As above, Black and White, Reverse Side Nickel, 50 cents.
No. 101 Dardevlet, Black and White, Reverse Side Nickel, 50 cents.
No. 201 Dardevle's Imp. Black and White, Reverse Side Nickel, 50 cents.
Similar Pattern as No. 15 except Black and White—Very Efficient.

proved more durable than wooden models. By the mid-1930s, most major manufacturers had converted their models to plastic. Collectors draw a definite line between the period a company built wooden plugs and the time they started making plastic models. Although plastic plugs have their place in the collectibles market, old wooden plugs are more valuable and more attractive to collectors.

Flies

As one of the oldest forms of artificial baits, flies and the art of fly tying have a rich history. In-depth descriptions of fly fishing and the process of tying flies, found in the writings of Berners and Walton, reveal that the art of tying flies was a deeply rooted tradition in Britain many centuries ago. Walton's instructions on how to tie flies, along with those of Charles Cotton published in Walton's fifth edition of *The Compleat Angler*, illustrate that the art has remained generally unchanged since the seventeenth century.

Like the contemporary fly fisherman or -woman, Walton and Cotton used a choice selection of hairs, furs, fabrics, and feathers to tie a variety of wet-fly patterns. In many cases, the anglers of the seventeenth and eighteenth centuries tied their flies to look like

The alluring lure box

Some lure boxes were better at catching anglers than the lures inside were at catching fish. The sales slogan that wins the day—although who can remember how many fish the lure actually caught—is for the Scandinavian Sockaroo by the Scandinavian Bait Company of Stillwater, Minnesota: "The bait with plenty of vim, vigor and viggle." These boxes are from the collection of Pete Press.

Night fishing

In the cool of the evening the walleye moves into shallow water to feed. This fine stringer was filled out with the help of Moonlight Bait Company's Crayfish, Heddon's Super Dowagiac Spook, Vamp and Baby Vamp, and a Flasher from the Long Island Manufacturing Company of Long Island City, New York. Memorabilia owner: Pete Press.

Trolling for heavy pike

Northern pike and muskies, the so-called "freshwater barracuda," were always a test of anglers and their tackle. The tasty lure at the end of this musky rod is a giant eight-inch (20-cm) James Heddon & Sons Vamp, made from 1925 to 1929. The jointed-body lure with single hooks resting on the boat's transom is a Tarpalunge made by the Shakespeare Bait Company of Kalamazoo, Michigan. The pine-wood tackle box by the Tronic Trunk Company had a water-tight gasket and was called the "Life Saving Box," as you could float with it if your fishing boat capsized. These pike and musky fishing items are from the collection of Arlen Carter.

specific insects, but they also tied generic flies that did not closely resemble any living thing. From that standpoint, fly tying has not evolved dramatically since Walton published his book. The use of color is one of the key differences between the trout flies of Walton's era and modern flies. Early fly fishermen placed an emphasis on how a fly behaved in the water, rather than on using bright colors or specific colors to attract fish. They also fished exclusively with wet-fly patterns.

The dry fly emerged in the nineteenth century. The first mention of dry-fly fishing appeared in third edition of *The Vade-Mecum of Fly Fishing for Trout* by George Philip Rigney Pulman of Britain, published in 1850. However, Pulman's mention of the dry fly did not make a significant impact on anglers. Not until Frederick Halford published his book *Floating Flies* in 1886 did anglers' attitudes toward the dry fly change. Halford's descriptions of dry-fly fishing dramatically changed the way anglers looked at flies. Many who read his book swore off the wet fly altogether and started fishing exclusively with dry flies.

Until the late 1800s, most American fly fishermen imitated British fly patterns. Gradually, however, Americans adapted their own fly patterns to fit the waters they fished. Theodore Gordon of New York was one of the major forces behind the changes in North American fly patterns. During the late 1800s and early 1900s, Gordon carefully studied trout and the entomology of streams. From his angling experiences, he developed new patterns of flies, such as the now-famous Quill Gordon, an early-season mayfly imitation. His contributions to the sport earned him titles such as the father of modern American angling and the father of American dry-fly fishing. Although he did not invent the dry fly, Gordon certainly helped to define it and popularize its use.

Other anglers followed Gordon's lead during the first half of the twentieth century. George M. L. La Branche, Edward R. Hewitt, Preston Jennings, Carrie Stevens, Ray Bergman, Charles Wetzel, Art Flick, and Lee Wulff each contributed their knowledge and research to the American style of fly tying.

Wulff, considered one of the greatest fly fishermen of the century, developed a variety of hair-wing flies, including the Royal Wulff, Black Wulff, and Grizzly Wulff, which remain standards in fly fishing today.

During the late 1800s and early 1900s, new patterns and styles of fly tying emerged in various regions of the United States. The first region to make significant contributions to fly tying was the Northeast. Anglers in New England, New York, and Pennsylvania began tying new forms of the wet fly in the mid-1800s. Many of their early creations were large and colorful flies used to attract the cooperative brook trout. As their focus turned toward imitating the natural foods of trout, they later introduced now-famous patterns like the Royal Coachman, Adams, and Light Cahill.

Southern anglers introduced the bass bug to fly fishing around

Chippewa Bait

This lure was produced circa *1915 by the Immell Bait Company of Blair, Wisconsin. Owner: Pete Press.*

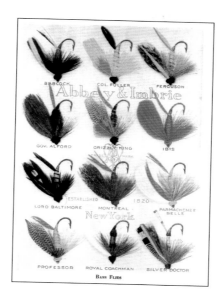

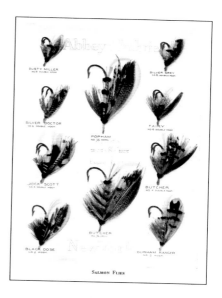

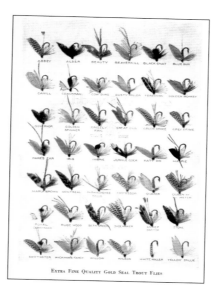

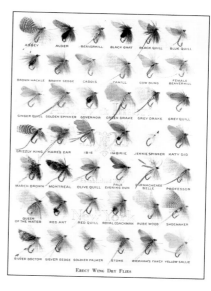

Above: **Commercial flies**

Numerous tackle manufacturers have offered commercially tied flies during the last one hundred years. This colorful selection appeared in Abbey & Imbrie's 1929 catalog.

Left: **Bass bugs**

Resting on these lily pads are bass bugs from Lauby, the Minnesota Bait Company, Shur-Luk, Peckinpaugh, N. G. Souther and Company, South Bend, Shakespeare, Moonlight, and Pflueger. Owner: Pete Press.

the turn of the century. Bass bugs are floating flies that typically represent frogs, mice, or minnows. Although he probably did not create the first bass bug, anglers routinely credit Ernest H. Peckinpaugh of Chattanooga, Tennessee, with inventing it during the first decade of the twentieth century, because he was a major force in shaping and defining the bait during its infancy. In the early years, anglers made bass bugs from balsa, cedar, or cork tied with feathers or deer hair, but later, bass bugs made from plastic and Styrofoam became popular commercial fly-fishing baits.

Of course, other regional anglers also contributed to North America's fly-tying tradition. The Northwest produced steelhead and salmon flies, while anglers in the Rocky Mountains developed their own styles of flies to match the conditions of their wild rivers. As saltwater fly fishing emerged, anglers created patterns to attract a vast array of ocean-dwelling species.

For collectors, the task of tracking down flies tied by famous fly fishermen is not easy, and authenticating such flies borders on the impossible. However, classic fly tiers had their own styles of tying just as famous decoy carvers had unique styles of painting and shaping their work, thus providing the avid collector with finger-prints to aid in the identification process. But while knowing the styles of well-known fly tiers helps in identifying and authenticating their work, most collectors of flies are content to simply own old flies or especially beautiful examples of classic patterns.

Collectors also search out commercial versions of flies, but they too can be difficult to identify. In the late nineteenth century, a number of commercial sources sold flies, including Pflueger and the T. H. Chubb Rod Company of Post Mills, Vermont. During the twentieth century, increasing numbers of companies dabbled in fly making. Some of their products are unmarked versions of familiar patterns, while others, such as the bass bugs produced by major tackle companies like Heddon, Creek Chub, Shakespeare, or South Bend, are unique and easier to identify.

Facing page: **Bass flies**
Fly fishing has intrigued fishermen and -women for centuries. These commercial flies and classic Meisselbach Expert reel are from the collection of Pete Press.

Chapter 4

Decoys

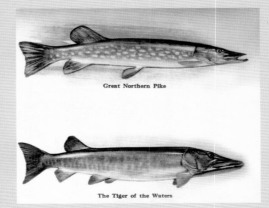

Great Northern Pike

The Tiger of the Waters

Main photo: **Spearfishing decoys**

Spearfishing is done in the cold of winter on ice in shallow bays, channels, and inlets. The decoys are used to draw in fish, which are then skewered by a spear such as the hand-forged one pictured here. Hand-crafted decoys of the 1930s and 1940s were colorful American folk art and effective fishing tools. These, made by Minnesota decoy carvers Charlie Stubbs, Leroy Howell, Elmer Lanski, Frank Mizra, Tom Barge, and Gerhard Behrens, are from the collection of Ron Adamson.

Inset: **Spearing for big game**

Both the northern pike and muskie were popular prey for spearfishermen and -women during the late 1800s and early 1900s. Spearfishing for muskies was eventually outlawed, but a few states such as Minnesota, Wisconsin, and Michigan still allow anglers to spear northern pike.

To the novice, a spearing decoy may seem nothing more than a lure without hooks, but collectors and spearfishermen and -women recognize the decoy as a distinct piece of angling equipment that has played a unique role in the history of fishing. Although some may argue that the decoy is the predecessor of the lure, these two types of bait have followed dramatically different evolutionary paths.

Both decoys and lures perform the similar task of attracting game fish by imitating prey and each claims certain artistic values. However, the lure is a tool of rod-and-reel anglers, produced mainly by commercial manufacturers. In contrast, the decoy is an instrument of spearfishermen and -women created almost exclusively by individual craftspeople who carry on a time-honored tradition through their work. While collectors sort lures by manufacturers and serial numbers, sorting decoys is not as easy, because in many cases the craftsperson's individual style is the only identifying mark. Geography also differentiates decoys from lures, because the use of decoys was, and remains, limited to a small region of North America that experiences the harsh realities of the northern winter. While anglers in these regions use decoys, other anglers could cast, troll, and jig lures throughout the waters of North America and the rest of the world.

The use of decoys can be traced back thousands of years to northeast Asia, where ancient spearfishermen and -women in what are now Siberia and Japan lured their prey with baits chipped and carved from materials such as stone, shell, and bone. As the Native Americans' ancestors traveled across the Bering Strait to North America, they carried with them the practice of spearfishing and decoy making. Archaeological work in Alaska unearthed examples of Eskimo decoys carved from ivory, bone, antler, and shell dating from 1000 to 500 B.C. Digs in the Great Lakes region also revealed decoys used by Native Americans thousands of years ago.

For Native American tribes inhabiting an area ranging from Alaska to Labrador, and south to Illinois and Nebraska, spearfishing was an important means of gathering food during the cold winter months. The basics of spearfishing with a decoy have not changed much through the centuries. Native American anglers would chop a hole through the ice and lie down near the opening, covering themselves with skins or branches to seal off outside light. After unraveling the sinew line from the jig stick, they lowered the decoy into the water. To attract fish, a series of jigging motions were used that made the decoy flutter or dance like an injured minnow, lively prey, or another game fish. When a target moved into range, the spear was thrown. A perfect strike hit the fish in the back of the head and paralyzed it. The angler then retrieved the fish by pulling in the line. Although it may not seem as efficient a method of taking fish as netting, a proficient spearfisherman or -woman could take home more than one hundred fish a day.

Early Native American decoy builders from tribes such as the

A thrill never forgotten

90

Ojibway, Sioux, Ottawa, Winnebago, and Menominee did not decorate their works with ornate carvings or designs. A decoy was a tool—quickly built, used, then discarded at the end of the spearfishing season when it was time to migrate to the spring camps. Simplicity equaled efficiency, and dominated the design of early Native American decoys—often they were no more than plain shapes carved from wood, shell, antler, or bone to imitate the silhouette of a fish. However, in order to produce a convincing lure, some builders painted their decoys, while others used charring to create markings. Feathers or leather affixed as a tail or fins gave the decoy additional realism, as did carved eyes, gills, and scales, and stones attached to the belly added weight to help provide balance. By the time European explorers and settlers arrived in the Great Lakes region, these decoy embellishments were common, and most tribes had adopted wood as their primary decoy-building material.

The immigrants who settled in what is now Minnesota, Wisconsin, Michigan, New York, and Ontario during the 1800s learned the art of spearfishing and decoy carving from the Native Americans. The adaptation of this practice by European settlers marked a milestone in the decoy's evolution. The infusion of different

The carvers

The wooden blanks and finished red and white spearing decoy were crafted by the husband and wife team of Oliver and Olga Reigstad of Duluth, Minnesota. Oliver would whittle the blanks while at his job, and Olga would then paint the decoys when he brought them home. The rare frog decoy pictured here was carved by John Tax. Owner: Carter Stenberg.

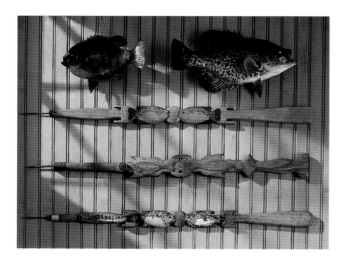

Above: **Kissing fish**

The ice-fishing sticks pictured here were created by William Faue. Faue carved most of his decoys, ice-fishing sticks, bobbers, and duck calls from the 1920s to the 1940s. From the collection of John Banholzer.

Right: **Copper baits**

These hand-hammered copper decoys were forged by Charlie Slechta, who created most of his work in the 1930s and 1940s. The most unusual piece pictured here is the three-headed decoy, known as an "egg-beater" decoy. The fisherman or -woman would wind his line with an egg beater, and as the line unwound, it would slowly spin the decoy in the water to attract fish. Owner: Dr. Gerald Wintheiser.

cultures' ingenuity, creativity, and personal expression on the basic Native American form pushed decoy carving into a new era of innovation and growth. Decoy carving was a tradition based on sustenance for Native Americans, but for European settlers it emerged more as a hobby and a commercial endeavor, which spawned some of the most unique and beautiful folk art ever created in the United States.

Builders selected easy-to-carve woods such as pine, cedar, poplar, or basswood for their decoy bodies. Intricate carving and painting produced both true-to-life replicas and flashy generic baits. Craftspeople built decoys in a variety of sizes, ranging from baitfish imitations a few inches long, to game fish replicas a few feet long. They poured molten lead into carved-out cavities in the belly for weight, improving on the stone-weight design used by Native Americans. Tin, leather, or copper fins strategically placed and bent stabilized the decoys and gave them added motion in the water. Glass and other shiny materials became eyes or were inlaid in the body to add bits of flash. Some builders used odds and ends like nails, rivets, shell casings, tobacco tins, and a wide variety of other objects to decorate their decoys. Immigrant anglers also improved on the Native American hanger design of drilling or burning holes in the decoy's back by adding screw loops or wire to which line could be attached. Some decoys had two or more hanger holes to vary the bait's position in the water. In addition to decoys resembling fish, builders also carved frogs, turtles, crayfish, muskrats, beavers, ducks, and other game-fish prey, in an attempt to imitate the natural foods of the fish.

Settlers also influenced aspects of spearfishing outside the art of decoy carving. They produced stronger, better-balanced spears made from iron that cut through the water with greater accuracy than the Native Americans' spears, which had wooden shafts with tips made from stone or wood. Immigrants also began using windowless wooden shacks as dark houses, which replaced the traditional skin or branch enclosures used by the Native Americans. Some spearfishermen even outfitted their shacks with stoves to improve the comfort level of winter angling.

By the mid- to late 1800s, spearfishing with decoys had evolved into a recreational pastime as well as a commercial business, with anglers pursuing muskies, northern pike, lake trout, sturgeon, and other game-fish species. Spearfishing drew small towns together and created temporary communities on the frozen surfaces of lakes and rivers. Within these communities, distinctive styles of decoy carving emerged, and the tradition of artistry forged by these early carvers is still carried on today in some areas.

Classic Traditions

The popularity of spearfishing and decoy carving escalated in the early 1900s and peaked during the depression in the 1930s. In the first half of the twentieth century, now-classic carvers produced beautiful decoys, which at the time sold for almost nothing, but today command thousands of dollars at auctions and sales. The great carvers each had a unique style that set them apart from the others, but theirs are not the only works valuable to collectors. Because they capture a moment in the sport's evolution and represent various individuals' styles and interpretations, even obscure decoys, created by now-forgotten craftspeople, sell for a great deal of money.

Among collectors, there is little argument over who the greatest decoy carver was. Oscar Peterson, a native of Cadillac, Michigan, produced thousands upon thousands of wonderful carvings in a career that spanned from the early part of the twentieth century until his death in 1951. Collectors admire Peterson for the realism he portrayed in his work. Whether it was a perch, muskie, or trout, the detail he captured set his work above that of other carvers. Although typically his carvings were not exact replicas of fish, his beautiful interpretations of them illustrated that decoy carving could truly be considered an art form. Whether it was the gentle curve of a tail or the uncanny facial features, a carving by Peterson almost threatens to come alive at any moment. Peterson's use of several layers of paints, metallic powders, and varnishes gave his work a bold presence and a natural finish. He often added touches of bright red in the mouth and gill openings, and when carving trout, he added attention-grabbing highlights of red to the belly, fins, or sides. Other features such as a wooden, backward-slanting tail and a streamlined shape also help collectors identify his work.

A MUSKIE IN ACTION

Peterson belongs to what has become known as the Michigan school of decoy carving. Like Peterson, other Michigan carvers were known for their realistic use of paint, which is especially evident in their trout decoys. Large decoys used on the Great Lakes, measuring more than a foot (3 m) in length, were common products of Michigan's artists. Carvers like Ken Brunning of Rogers City, Tom Schroeder of Detroit, Jim Nelson of Cadillac, and Hans Janner Sr., Gordon "Pecore" Fox, Yock Meldrum, and Gordon Frances Charbeneau of Mount Clemons, created wonderful works of art that typify the Michigan style.

The classic works created by Michigan artists were not the earliest examples of non–Native American decoy carving in North America. Spearfishermen in New England and the eastern Great Lakes states began perfecting their craft years before the art flourished in Minnesota, Wisconsin, and Michigan. The earliest style of decoy carving to emerge in the Great Lakes states was the New York or Lake Chautauqua school, which hit its peak between 1890 and 1900. Spearfishing and decoy making thrived in New York during the 1800s, especially in the Lake Chautauqua area. Commercial spearfishing was so heavy, however, that waters were quickly overfished. Pressure by conservationists forced a ban on the practice in New York, which went into effect during the first decade of the 1900s.

The one that didn't get away

This northern pike is unaware that the red and white fish he has in his sights is made of wood and will be his last mistake. The decoy at the "end of the line" was carved by John Tax (1894–1967) of Osakis, Minnesota. By trade, John was a guide, as well as a shoe and harness repairman. He also carved ducks, bird houses, and fish. Owner: Carter Stenberg.

New York spearfishermen typically carved decoys that measured less than eight inches (20 cm) in length. They painted their work with natural colors and markings. Common characteristics included a leather tail and fins, a hanger hole drilled in the top of the decoy, tack eyes, and a straight body. Because the balance of New York decoy carving occurred in the 1800s, surviving examples are difficult to come by today, and in most cases, the carvers' names remain unknown—lost or forgotten over time. Harry Seymour of Bemus Point is one of the few Lake Chautauqua carvers that collectors do know. He produced beautiful decoys during the late 1800s, the height of carving's popularity in New York. His work is not easy to find and commands very high prices.

Collectors classify Wisconsin carvers from the La Crosse area along the Mississippi River into another school of carving. Although just a segment of the work produced by Wisconsin carvers, the La Crosse decoys carried a specific style that was unique to this region. In addition to their quality and artisanship, La Crosse carvers set themselves apart by creating specialized decoys for river fishing. They typically painted their decoys with realistic markings that were more subdued than those found in carvings from other regions. Common characteristics included glass eyes, a wooden or metal tail and fins, and a straight body. The La Crosse decoys also tended to be rather small, measuring less than six inches (15 cm) in length. Outside the La Crosse area though, decoys of sturgeon were popular and have become a signature piece of Wisconsin carvers. Some of these decoys measure more than three feet (0.9 m) in length. The large size was a result of minimum-length restrictions. Carvers built their decoys to the exact length of the size limit so they could easily identify fish of legal size.

Across the Wisconsin border, Minnesota spearfishermen and -women established their own decoy-carving tradition. But unlike Michigan, Lake Chautauqua, or La Crosse carvings, it is not easy to link Minnesota decoys by common characteristics. While Minnesota decoys were usually rather small, measuring between four and nine inches (10–23 cm) in length, this is generally where the similarities between carvers' styles stopped. Their work varied dramatically, running the spectrum from natural-style decoys that imitated bait or game fish, to the abstract, which did not resemble any specific species of fish. Minnesota carvers also produced many ice decoys that were not fish, including diving ducks, mice, frogs, beavers, and tadpoles.

One of the most famous Minnesota carvers, whose work tends to lean toward the abstract, was Leroy Howell of Hinckley. He worked during the early to mid-1900s, producing plain, yet beautiful decoys. Howell commonly painted his decoys with one or two simple colors and created perfectly round eyes by tracing around a rifle shell. John Ryden of Aitken, another famous Minnesota carver, produced small, natural-colored decoys that he sold from his car during a sixty-year career. Other notable Minnesota carvers included Louie Leach of Fairmont, who often applied glitter to his decoys, Fred Lexow of Balsam Lake, Chet Sawyer of Duluth, and Frank Mizera of Ely.

The art of decoy carving was practiced in other states like Vermont, Pennsylvania, Indiana, and Illinois, but on a limited basis. The body of work that emerged from these states amounts to a trickle when compared to the flood of decoys produced by carvers in Michigan, New York, Wisconsin, and Minnesota.

Contemporary Carving

The unique carving style of the classic Native American tradition saw a rebirth of sorts in the twentieth century. Although the art of decoy carving had never stopped in Native American communities, it had waned during the end of the 1800s and beginning of the 1900s as immigrant Americans forced many tribes onto reservations and attempted to suppress their cultural practices and customs.

As the 1900s progressed, Native American decoy carving and spearfishing witnessed a resurgence as Native Americans began revisiting and relearning the traditions of their past. Collectors revere their work for its realistic beauty and distinctive style. Many carvers, such as those of Ojibway tribes in Minnesota and Wisconsin, continue to produce traditional minimalistic, all-wood carvings with no paint or markings just as their ancestors did hundreds of years ago. However, in an ironic circle of events, some contemporary Native American carvers have incorporated immigrant designs into their work. Metal fins, lead bellies, and tack eyes are all influences brought to the art by non–Native Americans.

Contemporary Native Americans continue to carve decoys and spear fish, carrying on the ancient tradition that influenced so many artists through the years. John Snow, of the Lac du Flambeau Ojibway in Wisconsin, is among the carvers who helped revitalize the art by producing wonderful and highly sought-after examples of Native American decoys. His work, and the work of others like him, helps to carry on one of the continent's oldest forms of cultural art.

Among non–Native Americans, spearfishing is a dying art carried on by a hearty few. Tight regulations on spearfishing have greatly reduced the number of anglers who participate in the sport and have diminished the demand for working decoys. However, the popularity of decoys as pieces of art among anglers and non-anglers alike has created a new market. Most collectors focus on antique decoys, but contemporary carvers also produce beautiful and respected examples of the craft. Guy Leslie of Marblehead, Ohio, is one of the most famous contemporary carvers. His highly respected work has gained national attention and continues to increase in value.

Unfortunately, forgers and artists who are out to make a quick buck have tried to cash in on the surge in the decoy's popularity. The result has been uncertainty among buyers and a wave of low-quality work that pops up in such places as souvenir and craft shops, flea markets, antique stores, and even tackle conventions. Because it can be very difficult to tell an antique from a forgery, collectors must do their research before buying any decoy.

Commercial Decoys

Many commercial decoys produced through the years represent half-hearted attempts by tackle manufacturers to tap into spearfisher-men's and -women's pocket books. A few companies did produce decoys that looked good and performed well. Most tackle manufac-turers avoided decoy production, or gave it limited attention, be-cause the market was small. Only anglers in the Great Lakes region speared fish through the ice, and most of them preferred to carve their own decoys or to buy decoys from local builders. Because of this, manufacturing and selling decoys was not a high priority for most tackle companies. They made more money by concentrating on lures, rods, reels, and other tackle with wider marketing potential.

Major tackle manufacturers like Heddon and Moonlight, both based in Michigan, did include decoys in their catalogs. Their busi-nesses sat in the heart of spearfishing country, and they understood the importance of the decoy in their region. In the early to mid-1900s, James Heddon's Sons of Dowagiac, Michigan, was the largest producer of commercial decoys. The company produced its wooden

Ice Minnow from 1913 through the 1920s. In the 1930s, Heddon replaced the Ice Minnow with the plastic-bodied Ice Spook. Most of the Heddon models measured less than five inches (13 cm) in length.

The Moonlight Bait Company of Paw Paw, Michigan, which became the Paw Paw Bait Company in the 1930s, was second to Heddon in commercial decoy production. Moonlight, and later Paw Paw, offered as many as three variations of their decoys in different colors, measuring seven inches (18 cm) or less in length. Other manufacturers including the South Bend Bait Company, the Creek Chub Bait Company, and the Pflueger Bait Company produced commercial decoys as well. Pflueger issued a soft rubber decoy in the 1890s and later built wooden versions.

Typically, commercial manufacturers offered one, two, or three models in different sizes and/or colors. In some cases, the decoys were the same models as the lures sold by the company, but without hooks. Manufacturers added metal fins and hangers, but the resulting product usually looked quite shoddy compared to hand-carved decoys. A few companies tried to make their decoys stand out from the rest by applying luminous paint or by adding flashy metal to their models. While some manufacturers produced wooden decoys, others used rubber, metal, and, later, plastic. Jay B. Rodes of Kalamazoo, Michigan, even built an aluminum model in 1919, which split in half to allow an angler to place lead weights inside. Needless to say, such decoys did not receive high praise from traditional spearfishermen.

A handful of regional companies, such as the Randall Decoys & Ice Spears Company of Willmar, Minnesota, experienced some success selling decoys in the early- to mid-1900s, but as states instituted tighter regulations on spearfishing in the mid- to late 1900s, commercial interest in the decoy market waned. A few states went as far as to outlaw spearfishing altogether, completely eliminating some markets.

Although many of the commercially produced decoys were not well received by spearfishermen, they have fared much better with collectors. In most cases, old factory-produced decoys, such as the models sold by Heddon, Moonlight, and Pflueger, are considerably harder to find than the lures made by those companies at the same time because of their limited production. When a collector does unearth a commercial decoy, it is usually a valuable find. Another factor that makes old commercial decoys attractive to collectors is the comfort of knowing who produced the model and when, which of course can be quite difficult with decoys built by individual craftspeople.

1927 Heddon trade catalog

The pyres of hell

This collection of hand-wrought spears was forged by various artisans over the past two centuries. From the collection of Ron Adamson.

Spearfishing Accessories

The quality of an angler's spear is as important as having an effective decoy in spearfishing. A good spear is balanced, solid, and sleek. The head is made from high-quality metal, has strong, sharp spines, and makes a reliable connection to the shaft. Although some people may claim that spears lack the artistic beauty of decoys, an experienced spearfisherman or -woman regards a quality spear as a fine piece of art.

Typically, spear heads are made in a traditional trident style with anywhere from three to nine spines. Anglers used larger heads, measuring in width from nine to twelve inches (23–30 cm), for big fish like sturgeon, northern pike, muskie, and lake trout. Small heads, with a width of three to five inches (8–13 cm), were used for perch, panfish, or whitefish. Spearing for walleyes, bass, or suckers required a head measuring six to eight inches (15–20 cm) in width.

Builders usually made the shafts out of wood, but they also used metals like brass, steel, and aluminum. Some spearfishermen and -women used their decoy-carving skills in their wooden-shaft design, not only to taper and balance, but to add subtle details as well. Designs could be as simple as a few turns on the lathe or as intricate as a hand-carved pattern. The length of the shaft depended on the depth of the water—anglers who speared in shallow water preferred shafts measuring three or four feet (0.9–1.2 m) in length, but deeper water required a shaft measuring five or six feet (1.5–1.8 m) in length. Some spears incorporated a breakaway head, which made the retrieval of fish easier. It was not uncommon for spearfishermen to use caps made from wood or rubber to protect the head when they transported or stored the spear.

Only a handful of tackle companies offered spears in their catalogs, so it is not easy to find surviving examples of commercial models. Many of the spears that collectors run across are homemade, making identification and dating nearly impossible. Some of the most respected spear builders, such as W. H. Kellog of Saginaw Bay, Michigan, did stamp their names on their spears, but in most cases, identifying marks are rare.

Although jigging sticks were often no more than a scrap of wood, some spearfishermen and -women took the time and effort to finish them with carvings or a turned handle. Usually, the design consisted of a single piece of wood bowed at either end to hold wound-up line on the stick. Another design featured a main stick with two small pieces of wood doweled to a side that line could be coiled around. In rare cases, anglers added a small reel to their jig stick for faster line retrieval.

Another collectible ice-spearing accessory is the dark-house box. Many spearfishermen and -women built boxes to hold their assortment of decoys, just as rod-and-reel anglers use tackle boxes to organize their lures. Some were nothing more than a converted toolbox or pail, while others resembled a miniature chest of drawers. As with other spearfishing tools, anglers sometimes painted and carved their dark-house boxes to give them a personal touch.

Although craftspeople continue to keep the art of decoy carving alive, the tradition of building spearfishing accessories is truly a dying art, because there is little or no contemporary market for them. A few anglers in states like Minnesota, Michigan, and Wisconsin continue to spear fish, but the sport is fading. If it disappears completely, the art of building spearfishing accessories may disappear as well.

The spearing house

This mint collection of William Faue decoys is illuminated by a stream of light coming through an open door. Faue, a carpenter and woodworker, created around one hundred spearing decoys a year and sold them for only fifty cents a piece in hardware stores. Owner: John Banholzer.

Chapter 5

Accessories

Main photo: **Bobbers, dobbers, and floaters**

Bobbers came in every shape, size, and color imaginable. While simple, they are also simply pleasing, American folk art at its best. This collage of bobbers is from the collection of Pete Press.

Inset: **Postcard *circa* 1940**

When the big ones are not biting, even the best lures and tackle offer little comfort. It is during such times that anglers must rely on their sense of humor to lighten an otherwise frustrating experience.

They included metal clips for hooks and flannel inserts that helped remove moisture from the flies and reduced mildew.

The late nineteenth century witnessed the popularization of fly boxes. As eyes became standard features on hooks, fewer anglers tied flies around the leader, which removed the need for leader storage space. These metal containers used compartments, loops, clips, and cork to hold and organize flies. Manufacturers sold a wide variety of boxes—some were round, while others were rectangular; some featured divided compartments or removable inserts; trout fly boxes had smaller compartments, while salmon fly boxes provided space for larger flies. During the twentieth century, more innovative versions emerged, like magnetized boxes that prevented flies from blowing away. Other models featured transparent lids on each compartment, a built-in magnifying glass, or a washable slate for labeling the box's contents.

Some companies also manufactured elegant, wooden fly boxes. These boxes or cabinets held an angler's complete collection of flies and usually remained at home. Hardy Brothers of England produced an exquisite model, built from teak and fitted with brass hardware, known as the Roxburgh fly cabinet. Fly cabinets typically came with removable trays or sliding drawers for easy access. Built primarily during the early 1900s for well-to-do fly fishermen, fly cabinets are unique and valuable collectibles.

The artificial lure boom of the late nineteenth and early twentieth centuries fueled the popularity of tackle boxes. Anglers needed plenty of space to hold their ever-increasing assortments of plugs, spinners, and spoons. Tackle boxes held dozens of lures and organized them neatly in divided compartments located in hinged or removable trays. They allowed anglers to easily transport their lures and accessories, and provided a safe storage space. Although a few commercial sources produced wooden tackle boxes, most companies used metals such as steel and aluminum before plastic found its way into tackle-box design.

During the 1800s and early 1900s, tackle companies issued various forms of fishing shirts and jackets for fly fishermen and -women. Specialized pockets made it easy to carry the vast array of equipment a fly fisherman or -woman needed on the stream. However, it was fly-fishing legend Lee Wulff who developed the fly vest, introducing it around 1930. The fly vest was light, convenient, and short enough to stay dry when wading in deep water. It typically had more than a dozen pockets of varying sizes, one or two wool pads to hold flies, and metal or plastic utility rings. Some even came equipped with zip-out creels. The vest's popularity grew quickly, and it soon became an invaluable piece of fly-fishing equipment.

Creels

Wicker creels crafted in the late nineteenth and early twentieth centuries have become sought-after treasures not only for collectors of antique fishing tackle, but also for those who just enjoy antiques.

Facing page: **Fly-fishing gear at the ready**

While anglers always hope that the fish will be biting and he or she will come home with a creel full of fish, it's never a bad idea to bring along a good book or two, such as The Idyl of the Split-Bamboo, *the rod-builder's handbook, written by Dr. George Parker Holden in 1920. Memorabilia owner: Pete Press.*

The unique character of creels makes them beautiful decorations for a house or cabin. During the last twenty years, they have evolved as pieces of antique Americana as familiar as spinning wheels, rug beaters, and lanterns. This has occurred to the displeasure of some collectors, who have witnessed the prices of creels skyrocket and have found it more difficult to track down desirable examples of the craft.

The concept behind the creel's development is fairly simple. When anglers bring in fish, they need a place to put their catch while also retaining their own mobility. Although not exclusively a tool of trout anglers, the creel is most often associated with trout fishing. Patrons of that sport commonly walk miles along a stream during a day of fishing, making the creel an ideal companion.

The first creel makers crafted their work from splints of willow, ash, or birch bark, which were chosen for their flexibility. They wove the splints together to create a box- or basketlike shape. On top was a lid or cover with an opening large enough to slide a trout through. Native Americans from the northeastern and northwestern regions of what is now the United States were making creels in this manner long before European settlers arrived, but they were not the only anglers to use them. Anglers in Europe have used creels for many centuries. Walton mentioned a creel, which he called a pannier, in *The Complete Angler*. Through the centuries, the creel evolved into the traditional basket-style creel that is so familiar to today's anglers. By the late nineteenth century, builders were producing intricate woven patterns with hinges and locking mechanisms—elements that are still a part of creel production today. Other builders made creels entirely out of leather or incorporated it into their designs as straps, locks, bottoms, or covers to make their creels more durable. One popular nineteenth-century version of the creel was a wooden box that doubled as a stool.

The desire to create a lighter, more compact creel in the twentieth century led to the use of flax or other types of canvas and cloth in creel design. Later, creels made from aluminum and synthetic materials such as vinyl, plastic, and rubber entered the marketplace as manufacturers attempted to create easy-to-clean models with better insulation and ventilation.

For collectors, identifying who built a creel is an almost impossible task in many cases. Most wicker creels built by individual craftspeople during the 1800s and early 1900s carry no identifying marks. Even factory-built creels produced during the first half of the twentieth century rarely carried tags, names, or product numbers. Two manufacturers that did mark their creels were the George Lawrence Company and W. H. McMonies & Company, both of Portland, Oregon. They were among the largest producers of quality

"A true fish story"

A 1912 postcard of a California angler and his catch shows a typical wicker creel design from the early decades of the twentieth century. The illustration reveals that possession limits were quite liberal or not yet established in California when this angler posed with his stringer of more than fifty trout.

wicker creels in the early 1900s, and because their creels are identifiable, they are highly prized by collectors. Other important manufacturers included the E. P. Peters Company and the John Clark Saddelery Company, also from Oregon, and Hardy Brothers of England. Many of the United States's creel manufacturers were forced to close their doors in the mid-1900s because they could not compete with a flood of cheaply produced Asian creels that were being imported to North America. As a result, the majority of desirable commercial models were built prior to the 1950s.

Stringers and Fish Baskets

While trout fishermen advanced the development of the creel, anglers who pursued larger game-fish species cultivated their own accessories for holding fish, called stringers and fish baskets.

With the creel, the trout angler had mobility and space enough to hold a limit. But for anglers who fished for northerns, muskies, or walleyes, the creel was useless—they needed a tool to carry big fish. The accessory that emerged was the stringer. The first and simplest form of a stringer was a Y-shaped tree branch, which some anglers (especially kids) still use today. The mechanics of the stringer were very basic—one side of the Y-shaped branch was snapped off near the intersection, fish were strung on the opposite side through their gills and mouth, and the stub end of the broken side served as a stop to hold the fish on the branch.

Commercial stringers appeared in the late 1800s and became a staple in tackle manufacturers' catalogs in the 1900s. One of the most popular models was simply a thin rope measuring about three or four feet (0.9–1.2 m) in length that had a sharp metal piece resembling a large needle on one end and a metal loop connected to the opposite end. An angler pushed the needle through the fish's gill opening or the soft underside of the mouth to thread it onto the rope. After slipping the first fish on the stringer, the angler doubled the needle back through the loop to prevent the fish from sliding off.

Another model popularized during the early to mid-1900s was the snap-hook stringer which was a metal chain or piece of heavy wire with a half-dozen or more snap hooks evenly spaced along its length. For the angler who felt they would be sure to catch and keep more than six or eight medium to large fish, some companies, like James Heddon's Sons, offered add-on hooks. Rust was a common enemy to the all-metal snap-hook models, but the emergence of better materials reduced or eliminated corrosion. Manufacturers introduced stringers made from aluminum alloys, and later, rubber-coated stringers and models made entirely from plastic appeared on the market.

Pflueger fish stringer

During the first half of the twentieth century, most of the major tackle companies offered a variety of accessories, which supplemented the sale of lures, rods, and reels. This 1928 Pflueger catalog ad illustrates the company's E-Z-Off Fish Stringer.

Wire fish baskets also gained popularity during the early to mid-1900s. They were similar to creels in that they could only hold smaller fish, but the baskets differed because they allowed anglers to keep their fish alive. Manufacturers constructed these baskets with paper-clip-thin lengths of aluminum that were woven together to create a collapsible basket shape. On top was a spring-loaded cover that opened downward into the basket. It allowed anglers to slip their catch into the basket without removing the basket from the water. Some models featured a spring-loaded trap door on the bottom, which opened outward to make the fish easier to remove. In the mid-1900s, manufacturers began equipping their baskets with a foam ring that encircled the top of the basket to keep it afloat.

While useless for larger game-fish species like northerns or walleyes, because they were typically no more than twelve to twenty inches (30–50 cm) wide, fish baskets were and continue to be common accessories used by panfish anglers. Some anglers prefer them over stringers because they are easier on fish and provide a better survival rate if fish are released.

Although anglers still use stringers and fish baskets today, increasing numbers of anglers now equip their boats with live wells, which can hold larger fish and greater numbers of fish, while keeping them alive with aeration systems.

1930s tall-tale postcard

Landing Nets

The practice of using nets to land fish caught with a rod is as old as the sport of fishing. Unlike casting nets or seines, the landing net does not actually catch the fish, but aids an angler in bringing the fish to the boat or to shore.

The size, type, and quality of landing nets vary widely. Early on, builders crafted their nets with wooden frames and handles. This practice continues today with some companies—Orvis, for example, still produces wooden models for anglers who appreciate beautiful landing nets.

The process of building a wooden landing net has not changed dramatically since the nineteenth century. Builders bend and shape or cut woods such as walnut, cherry, and ash to create the familiar circular or triangular bow, and smooth, straight handle. When the frame is complete, they drill holes along the edges of the bow and attach the netting or tie the netting to the bow. In rare cases, builders carve designs on the frame. An application of varnish or other finish protects the wood from wear and the elements.

In the twentieth century, manufacturers incorporated a variety of materials, including steel, aluminum, and plastic, in frame design. Stronger and more resilient materials such as nylon and rubber replaced cotton string and waterproofed silk as netting material.

The sizes of landing nets cross the spectrum. A small fly-fishing net may have a bow measuring less than a foot (0.3 m) across, equipped with a short handle and a French clip, which attaches to a fly vest. In contrast, big-game anglers who fish for muskies, northerns, salmon, or saltwater species, use mammoth nets measuring a few feet across the bow, with handles five- or six-feet (1.5–1.8 m) long.

Through the landing net's evolution, manufacturers experimented with ways to make their nets easier to carry. They built models with handles that folded, telescoped, or screwed on, or equipped their nets with collapsible bows.

Gaffs

Like the landing net, anglers developed the gaff to help lift large fish into a boat or onto shore. Although not commonly used in modern freshwater angling, the gaff remains a valuable tool for saltwater anglers and a few freshwater anglers who pursue giant catfish, salmon, or other species too large to fit in a landing net. Gaffs were once common equipment for anglers who wanted to lift large muskies or northerns into their boats. However, because releasing such fish is a common practice today and the gaff does not allow for this, most anglers would frown on anyone who used a gaff on either of these species.

Although it is nothing more than a metal hook connected to a pole, an old gaff certainly makes an interesting addition to an antique tackle collection. The gaffs used during the 1800s and early 1900s had hooks cast from iron or steel that were connected to wooden or cane poles of ash or bamboo. In some cases, builders simply pushed the hook into the hollow bamboo, but higher-quality models used rivets or ferrules to hold the connection. A few manufacturers, such as Hardy Brothers, went the extra mile by building telescoping metal handles or by working wooden handles on a lathe. As technology improved in the twentieth century, builders began using lighter, more rust-resistant metals such as stainless steel and aluminum in both hook and pole construction. Aluminum spawned light, compact versions that assembled quickly and fit in a tackle box.

Priests

Since prehistoric times, anglers have used various forms of the priest to restrain or kill fish. The first priests were simply the sturdiest objects within reach. Anglers often hit a fish on the head with a stick or rock to knock it unconscious. As fishing equipment evolved, priests became better defined as clubs of various lengths and

"Land the BIG ones"
By the 1940s, many tackle companies had begun using aluminum in gaff construction because it was light, durable, and resisted corrosion. This 1946 advertisement is for the three-piece Master Gaff built by the Wil-Sel Products Company of Chicago.

weights. The exact origin of the tool's name is uncertain, but it is likely a reference to a clergyperson's duty of administering last rites.

During the fishing-tackle boom of the late 1800s, manufacturers began offering priests in their catalogs. Priests remained common catalog items through the mid-1900s. The growing practice of catch-and-release angling drastically reduced the popularity of priests, but a few companies still offer them.

During the peak of their popularity, priests came in a variety of sizes and shapes. Hardy Brothers, for example, offered a salmon priest and a scaled-down version called the trout priest. Wooden models dominated the market in the early years, but later, versions made from stainless steel and aluminum replaced the traditional wooden priests. To make their priests more enticing to anglers, manufacturers occasionally incorporated other fishing tools, like gaffs and hook disgorgers, into their designs.

Most valuable to the collector are the beautifully carved and finished wooden models, as well as more unique examples built with brass, chrome, and even ivory, which suited the taste of the aristocratic angler.

Floats

A float, or bobber, serves a dual purpose in angling. Whether constructed from cork, wood, plastic, or foam, or whether it slips or is stationary, the function of the bobber is basically the same. Most bobbers allow an angler to float a bait at a specific depth and change the depth quite easily. In most cases, floats also alert an angler to a strike from a fish.

The shapes, sizes, and colors of bobbers vary dramatically to fit water conditions, light availability, and the type of fish being pursued. A bobber can range from a tiny piece of colored yarn tied to a fly fisherman's line, to something resembling a plastic softball. The variations produced over the years by hundreds of companies cover a broad spectrum that has evolved from two simple types of floats: the quill and the cork.

Using a bobber is not a modern angling innovation—the oldest known illustrations of floats date back to the fifteenth century and depict floats of various sizes made from cork. In the eighteenth and nineteenth centuries, anglers commonly built their floats from cork or quills. Quills from geese, ducks, and porcupines were popular float materials for centuries. In the case of waterfowl quills, anglers cut off the section from the tip to where the feathers started. They cleaned out the inner portion of the quill, then sealed the open end with pitch. To improve the float's visibility, anglers attached a piece of cotton to the quill. Although effective with light baits and tackle, the quill float's size limited the amount of weight it could hold. Quill floats were also better suited for use on the quiet water of lakes or ponds because they had problems staying afloat in the heavy current of a river or on breezy days when waves blew across the surface of a body of water.

Abbey & Imbrie floats

Illustrations from a 1910 Abbey & Imbrie catalog show the company's selection of floats. They were made from both cork and porcupine quills.

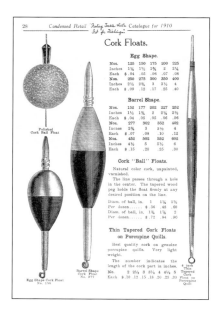

For anglers working with heavier bait and equipment, a cork float was a common choice because anglers could easily cut it into a wide range of sizes. Once an angler had cut the cork to a desired size and shape, a hole was burned through the center with a piece of hot metal wire so that line could be fed through it. An angler was able to secure the float at a specific depth by doubling the line through the hole and around the float, or by sticking a stop in the hole. Cork floats were preferred by anglers who fished rivers or streams, because they could remain buoyant even in heavy currents.

During the late nineteenth and early twentieth centuries, tackle manufacturers produced countless variations of the bobber. There were round bobbers, thin bobbers, bobbers that tied on line, and bobbers with metal hooks or clips that connected to line. Some

Folk art

This ice fishing box was made by Courtney "C. W." Quandt (1886–1961) of Red Wing, Minnesota. His drop lines were hand crafted, his bobbers made from bottle corks, and his ice skimmer—whether from necessity or just the love of fishing—was made by drilling holes into a small frying pan and then screwing it to a broom handle. Fishermen like Mr. Quandt used both care and ingenuity in creating the tackle they used to land their favorite fish. Memorabilia owner: Jerry Grayling.

"Hopper Coop"

Cricket boxes came in a variety of shapes and sizes. This illustration depicts a metal box called the "Hopper Coop." A sliding lid on top gave an angler controlled access to his insects, while perforated sides provided oxygen for the bait.

Magic minnow bucket

By the 1930s, the two-piece metal minnow bucket was a common item in tackle manufacturers' catalogs. An angler could buy a basic model for about one dollar in 1930. For a few dollars more, he or she could purchase a floating model, or one with an air-fed system, which represented the latest advancement in minnow bucket technology at the time.

bobbers came with wooden stops and others had built-in, spring-loaded stops. The most desired by collectors are the beautiful, hand-painted, wooden models. Manufacturers used colors like red, white, green, and yellow or combinations of colors to increase the visibility of the bobber when it floated on the water—as well as to catch the angler's eye at the sporting goods store.

The main problem for collectors is that old bobbers, especially those from the 1800s, are extremely difficult to find. When a collector does find an antique bobber, it is often hard to identify the manufacturer and pinpoint the year of production. Many bobbers did not have labels or serial numbers, so their origin remains a mystery; but some of the major tackle manufacturers that produced bobbers, such as Heddon, used company advertisements or patent numbers that help today's collectors identify their various models. As it is with many accessories, however, the fun in collecting old bobbers lies more in owning a piece of angling history than in collecting them for their monetary value or because of the manufacturer who built them.

Bait Containers

Stopping at a bait store to buy a carton of night crawlers or a dozen minnows seems a trivial part of a fishing trip today, but for anglers of the eighteenth and nineteenth centuries, using live bait was a chore. Anglers first had to catch, dig up, or trap their bait. Then they had to figure out a way to transport it. Night crawlers were easy enough to transport, but minnows, leeches, and bugs were a different story.

Anglers could put their minnows or leeches in a bucket, but the water was easily spilled and leeches could escape without some type of cover. Minnows and leeches also needed fresh water or they would not survive for very long. Anglers battled with these problems until tackle manufacturers began producing various forms of the minnow bucket.

The basic design was simple. The bucket came in two parts—the outer portion was a solid metal bucket and the inner portion was a perforated bucket with a hinged cover. When an angler removed the inner bucket, the water drained into the outer bucket and the minnows were easily accessible. The design also allowed for submersion of the bucket, which permitted fresh water to enter without losing the minnows. Manufacturers also sold one-piece buckets with perforated lids that worked just as well.

The mid-1900s witnessed the introduction of minnow buckets fitted with synthetic foam, which added buoyancy. Eventually, plastic and Styrofoam buckets replaced the traditional metal models. Late-twentieth-century technology added heaters and aeration systems. But for today's collectors, the most prized minnow buckets are the old, metal models painted with the manufacturer's name and logo, like those produced by the Old Pal Company of Lititz, Pennsylvania.

Another type of bait container is the cricket basket. Although rarely used today, the cricket basket, or bait cage, provided anglers with an easy way to carry bugs such as grasshoppers or crickets. The basket's design commonly included a base, two sides, and a top made from wood or metal, and wire screen that covered the two remaining sides. The basket opened from the top or side. Some bait cages were tubular in shape with a cone top and had a door, screw cap, or cork stop that covered their openings. The most valuable forms of baskets feature painted wood or a unique design that reflects the amount of care put into the piece by its builder.

Lines

Fishing line is not an item most collectors regularly seek out. Part of the disinterest lies in the extreme difficulty in identifying a line's manufacturer. Others shy away from it because it lacks the artistic expression that can be found in other forms of tackle. Because line is such a disposable item, it also becomes difficult to track down surviving examples of antique lines, especially those from the nineteenth century. Line certainly is not a collectible that boasts hoards of admirers, yet it has played an important role in the evolution of fishing.

Until the mid-1800s, horse hair was the predominant material used in line construction. Most anglers preferred white and gray stallion hairs, but their color choices varied with water conditions. Light colored hair was used in clear water, and darker hair was preferred for murky water. In some cases, anglers even dyed the hair to match the water color. A single horse hair had the breaking strength of an approximate two-pound (0.9-kg) test. Anglers braided hairs together to create the desired strength but ran into problems with horse-hair line, because it became bulky when they wove too many strands together.

In the mid-1800s, lines made from silk worm gut became more readily available to American anglers. Most were imported from Spain. These lines proved popular because they were much stronger than an equal diameter of horse-hair line, with strengths that tested at ten to fifteen pounds (4.5–6.8 kg) or more. Silk gut remained one of the predominate line materials well into the 1900s.

The twentieth century saw the introduction of thread linen line and, later, braided nylon line. Both proved stronger and more durable than horse-hair or silk line. Following World War II, DuPont introduced nylon monofilament line to the fishing world. It revolutionized the sport, because it was lighter and far less visible than any line previously produced. It provided anglers with the powerful new tool of

"Swell Lines for any Reel"

Prior to the introduction of nylon, braided silk lines were the industry norm. This advertisement for Rain-Beau Fishing Line promotes braided, silk fly line that was impregnated with oil to keep it soft, pliable, and afloat. Regular applications of line dressing were required to clean and lubricate such lines.

near-invisibility, which made catching fish much easier. It also offered increased strength at the fraction of the weight of other lines. Synthetic lines helped popularize the spinning reel and added new freedoms to other forms of fishing. Synthetic fly lines did away with line dressing and added new selections of lines like tapered and weight-forward lines that allowed fly fishermen or -women to fine tune their angling techniques. Synthetic lines continue to improve as technology develops stronger, lighter, and more durable materials.

The art of making horse-hair line is kept alive today by a few anglers who enjoy using the bait and tackle of earlier centuries. Dressing up in the clothing worn by anglers of the eighteenth and nineteenth centuries, they fish with the rods and reels of the time and even use homemade horse-hair line in many cases. Their attention to detail in the re-creation of angling practices from centuries past gives them a unique glimpse into the time and effort fishing's progenitors took to put line on a rod and reel.

"Move Up to a Mercury Cruiser"

The Mercury motor, produced by Wisconsin's Kiekhaefer Corporation, established a reputation as one of America's best outboards during the middle decades of the twentieth century.

Outboard Motors

A Wisconsin motor builder named Ole Evinrude forever changed the fishing world in the first decade of the twentieth century. Evinrude developed the first commercially successful gasoline outboard motor in 1909 at his shop in Milwaukee and received his first patent in 1910. His one-cylinder motor weighed sixty-two pounds (28 kg) and sold for sixty-two dollars. The motor quickly captured international attention as anglers everywhere clamored to buy one. Evinrude's product provided anglers with a new technological advantage and helped start a revolution in the outboard motor industry. Although Evinrude's motor was not the first gas-powered outboard, it was the first to achieve widespread commercial success.

A few gasoline outboards appeared before Evinrude's motor. Historians believe that the American Motor Company of Long Island City, New York, built and sold the first gasoline outboard in 1896, but collectors have yet to find a surviving example. The mass-produced Waterman Porto built by the Waterman Marine Motor Company of Detroit, Michigan, went into production in 1905 and became the first motor advertised as an "outboard motor." The Submerged Electric Motor Company of Menomonie, Wisconsin, started producing an electric outboard in 1900 and came out with a short-lived gasoline outboard in 1906. It was Evinrude's motor, however, that popularized the outboard. Because his design was reliable, practical, and affordable, it encouraged other builders to join the market. Anglers could not wait to buy an outboard, and manufacturers scrambled to imitate the design, trying to capture a share of this fledgling industry. Some motors produced in the 1910s, like the privately produced Motorgo sold by Sears, Roebuck, and Company of Chicago, Illinois, and the Hiawatha sold by Montgomery Ward & Company, also of Chicago, became popular, while other brands came and went. In the years that followed, companies like the Johnson Motor Company of South Bend, Indiana, and the Kiekhaefer Corporation of Cedarburg, Wisconsin, which made Mercury motors, became household names as they provided generations of anglers with quality outboard motors. During the middle decades of the 1900s, dozens of other companies, including the Champion Outboard Motors Company and Scott-Atwater Outboard Motors of Minneapolis, Minnesota; Martin Motors of Eau Claire, Wisconsin; and Oliver Outboard Motors of Battle Creek, Michigan, made their mark on the industry.

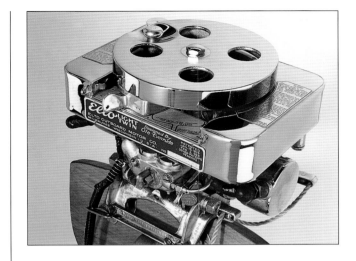

Collectors who belong to the Antique Outboard Motor Club often boast substantial collections of motors. They commonly restore their old motors to near-new working condition and put their collectibles to use. But because motors take up so much space, most tackle collectors are content to own a few smaller, low-horsepower motors.

As with other fishing collectibles, the prices of antique outboard motors vary widely, but abundant models or those with name recognition tend to sell for higher prices than some rarer models. There are exceptions, like the Imperial, produced by Fred and Robert Valentine of Minneapolis, Minnesota, around 1900. Their outboard predated Evinrude's motor and would surely command a dizzying price, but collectors have yet to find one.

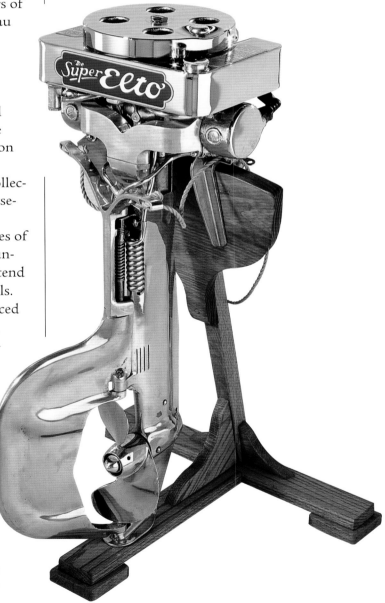

Both photos: **The Super Elto**

This motor, designed by Ole Evinrude himself, was produced by the Elto Outboard Motor Company of Milwaukee, Wisconsin, in 1926. The light-twin, Super-G, 4-hp motor, owned by John Keenan, is in mint condition.

Above: **"Hush-a-bye quiet"**

When Ole Evinrude built his first gasoline outboard in 1909, the motor's reliable design alone prompted anglers all over the world to buy one. When this advertisement appeared in 1954, tough competition from other companies forced Evinrude Motors to make creative claims in order to sell its products.

Right: **The boat house**

Pictured here is a 1918 Evinrude rowboat motor on the transom of a boat produced by Minnetonka Boat Works in 1917. Owner: John Keenan.

The workshop

Pictured here are a 2.5-hp 1941 Johnson Sea-Horse and a 1927 model from the Lockwood-Ash Motor Company of Jackson, Michigan. Owner: John Keenan.

Knives

Every angler at one time or another has used a knife while fishing and probably routinely carries one when on an angling excursion. Although knives are unquestionably an ancient tool, those marketed specifically to anglers have been around since the 1920s. Anglers have carried a wide variety of knives, ranging from fillet knives to combination knife/tools in their tackle boxes, boats, and fly vests. Some fishing knives are simple, while others are complex. A few are truly beautiful creations. The quality of knives varies widely from the cheap and unreliable to hand-crafted models that will last many lifetimes.

Anglers of the mid-nineteenth century used multi-purpose knives for their fishing needs. Usually these were large knives resembling the well-known bowie knife. Smaller knives with blades measuring four or five inches (10–13 cm) in length became available after the turn of the century. The specialization of fishing knives began after World War I, when a knife maker named William W. Scagel of Muskegon, Michigan, started producing knives for specific fishing needs. Among his developments was the fillet knife, which had a long, narrowly tapered blade that made cleaning fish easier. His work inspired fishing tackle manufacturers to produce their own lines of fishing knives and combination knife/tools. Other notable producers from the first few decades of the 1900s included the W. R. Case & Sons Cutlery Company of Little Valley, New York; the Remington Arms Company of Bridgeport, Connecticut; and the Marble Safety Axe Company of Gladstone, Michigan.

The sizes and variations of the combination knives are too many to count. In addition to the knife or knives, most include other tools like files, screwdrivers, hook removers, scalers, hook sharpeners, corkscrews, scissors, pliers, or countless other gadgets. Case even built a model with a built-in gaff. Manufacturers have used a wide variety of materials in blade and handle construction, including aluminum, brass, stainless steel, bone, ivory, and plastic. Many knives fold down into compact shapes that fit in a pocket or hang from a belt.

A whole host of other individual fishing accessories came and went over the years, such as fly vises, ice augers, depth finders, scissors, clamps, scalers, minnow scoops, and hook removers. Most are available at collectors shows, flea markets, antique stores, and over the Internet. While they generally have limited monetary value, their unique characteristics add a bit of color to a collection. They also stand as wonderful examples of the imagination and ingenuity that tackle manufacturers have used to lure both fish and consumers. Each is an important piece in the giant puzzle of fishing's evolution. 🐟

"Amazing!"

This 1952 advertisement for the Johnson Sea-Horse 3 claimed the motor's angle-matic drive allowed it to ski over underwater obstructions without damage to the lower unit. How many anglers would like to test that claim with their new outboard?

Chapter 6

Art and Literature

Main photo: **The sporting goods store**

This fishing tackle display from the Winchester Repeating Arms Company of New Haven, Connecticut, is reminiscent of what you might have seen if you were window shopping in the 1920s. Winchester manufactured and commissioned other manufacturers to produce fishing tackle from 1919 to 1931. Memorabilia owner: Carter Stenberg.

Inset: **Catalog illustrations**

These illustrations from the back cover of a 1932 South Bend catalog represent some of the extraordinary fishing artwork created for advertisements during the first half of the twentieth century.

When a collector turns the crank of an Edward vom Hofe reel and feels its gears and spool glide in the smooth rhythm of precision, or when an angler runs a hand along the splendid finish of an H. L. Leonard fly rod and relishes its fine-tuned elegance, it becomes clear that these objects are something more than fishing tools; they are, in all respects, pieces of art. Many of the rods, reels, and lures created over the course of angling's history are expressions of the labor and love of their makers. They suggest that fishing is more than a simple sport; it is an artistic tradition of sorts, continually evolving as new craftspeople contribute their vision to angling's rich fabric.

Other forms of art, however, apart from the tools of fishing, crisscross that fabric as over the years artists and writers have attempted to capture the sport's essence with paintbrush and pen. The artwork and literature that they have left behind opens a window through which we can view the thoughts, trends, and ideas of generations past. They provide a look into fishing's evolution and remind us how little our experiences differ from those of anglers centuries ago. In its basic form, fishing remains a simple sport, yet the web of art and literature it spawned is a rich, complex tapestry of colorful work, which reflects the ancient battle between man and fish.

Old fishing art and literature holds a special place in the hearts of collectors, who value it for its historical merits, beauty, uniqueness, and research potential. The scope of fishing art and writing covers a vast field of works ranging from eighteenth-century oil paintings and books to the sketches and descriptions of lures in a twentieth-century commercial catalog. Each collector values a particular type of art or writing for different reasons, but most are in agreement that all of these works are important pieces in the evolution of the angling tradition. To own a slice of that tradition enables a collector to grasp and hold on to a moment in time, while gaining a greater understanding of how anglers of previous generations perceived the sport.

Brook trout

The beauty of trout and the romantic nature of fly fishing have inspired generations of artists to draw or paint scenes like this one: a Currier & Ives lithograph, circa 1880, depicting a hooked brook trout struggling against an angler's line.

Paintings

For centuries artists have attempted to capture the emotion of angling and the beauty of game fish through a wide variety of mediums ranging from oil and water-color paintings to pencil sketches. Early wildlife and landscape artists did not concentrate exclusively on fishing, however. Often, fishing was just one topic touched on by artists during their careers.

Although the portrayal of fishing in art dates back thousands of years to ancient cultures, such as those of the Egyptians and Chinese, the modern era of fishing art began in seventeenth-century Britain. The first artist to concentrate on sporting art was a British painter named Francis Barlow. Through his etchings and oil paintings, he attempted to capture the sporting life of his homeland, producing works depicting fish and other wildlife. During the 1700s, paintings of fish and fishing gained a following in Britain, but paintings of hunting and horses were far more popular. It was not until the 1800s that fishing artwork gained higher acceptance in both Britain and the United States. Angling-related works became important cultural expressions on both sides of the Atlantic, and their popularity continues today.

Winslow Homer, one of the most highly regarded painters in American history, helped fishing paintings gain greater esteem during the nineteenth century. Although Homer is most well known for his paintings of the sea, he was an avid fisherman and used watercolors to capture fishing scenes set in the Adirondacks.

Paintings of anglers and fish cross many genres. Artists have depicted fish and fishing in landscapes, naturalistic portrayals, caricatures, portraits, and still lifes. All make a statement about angling in a particular era. They reveal the advancements and trends in the sport through their representation of tackle and equipment. They teach historians and collectors about the evolution of fishing and show how anglers who fished decades or centuries ago practiced and perceived the sport.

As is the case with most fishing collectibles, the value of a painting weighs heavily on who created it and when. Certainly paintings from the eighteenth and even nineteenth centuries are out of the reach of the average collector's pocketbook, but a great number of twentieth-century paintings and prints are affordable. Contemporary American artists, like Norman Browne, have found a healthy market for their paintings of fish and fishing, and such works remain hot commodities in art galleries. Especially popular today are paintings of fly fishing, flies, and trout.

The paintings produced for trout and salmon stamps, which accompany fishing licenses in some states, are also

Leaping bass

Sherman Foote Denton's 1889 painting of a fly fisherman fighting a bass provides a detailed view into the world of nineteenth-century angling.

popular collectibles, especially at the local level. But although they are sought-after items in their respective states, they have not gained a strong following nationwide. Sporting goods retailer Abercrombie & Fitch of New York City attempted to issue a National Fish Stamp in 1974, but the stamps did not create enough interest and were discontinued after two years.

Books

Anglers' undying thirst for knowledge drives a seemingly endless market for fishing-related books. The scope of such works ranges from journals to technical manuals to tales of adventure, and from fiction to nonfiction. Each aims at attracting a piece of a massive audience that buys and devours books with an insatiable appetite.

While the hunger for new angling literature remains high, collectors also reach out for the classics—attempting to grasp a piece of fishing's history by owning timeless words that have captured the thoughts and imaginations of anglers for generations. Through these classic pieces of literature, modern anglers are able to put their places in the sport's evolution into perspective. They learn from the experimentation and discoveries that guided the anglers before them. Fishing is a fluid sport that perpetually grows and evolves to meet the needs of the present. This fluidity becomes evident while reading old fishing books; such stories inadvertently serve as narrators for the story of fishing's development. Yet with all the changes and advancements the sport has seen through the centuries, anglers' love for fishing has remained the same, and this, too, is evident when reading classic angling books.

One of the most memorable and highly acclaimed books ever written on fishing is Izaak Walton's *The Compleat Angler*, which was first published in 1653. Finding an early edition of Walton's book is next to impossible, but collectors may run across a later edition published in the nineteenth or twentieth centuries. Other important English works also emerged in the 1600s, including Thomas Barker's *The Art of Angling* and Colonel Robert Venables's *The Experienced Angler*, but collectors are not likely to find early editions of these either. More realistic acquisitions are the angling books published in the 1800s and 1900s.

Works such as Thaddeus Norris's *The American Angler's Book*, Robert Barnwell Roosevelt's *Superior Fishing*, and *Frank Forester's Fish and Fishing*, by Henry William Herbert, are just a few of the

"Fish and Fishermen I have known"

The telling of a fishing tale is captured in this cover image from a 1924 Shakespeare brochure.

significant American fishing books written during the nineteenth century.

During the 1900s, the market for angling books exploded, and publishers rushed to fill the demand. The result is a long line of titles, some valuable to collectors, others just forgotten footnotes in the stream of angling literature. It is not always certain what collectors will want, however. *A River Runs Through It*, by Norman Maclean, was a rather quiet collection of short stories for nearly twenty years until Robert Redford turned the title story into an acclaimed motion picture. Suddenly, collectors were clamoring for copies of the book, and its collectible value rose dramatically.

For collectors of fishing books, sorting out what is collectible and what is not seems a monumental task in the early stages, but, as is the practice with other collectibles, people usually find an area of concentration and stick with it. Pricing can also be difficult and takes some significant research. Value usually depends on the age, the edition, the author, and the number of copies printed, although every old book is not necessarily worth a great deal of money. Signed copies and first editions tend to command higher prices as well. A signed first edition of George M. L. La Branche's classic *The Dry Fly and Fast Water* from 1914 would sell for more than $100, while an updated edition from the 1950s is worth a small fraction of that price.

Flea markets, antique stores, library sales, and used bookstores are good places to look for old fishing books, but when searching out a hard-to-find title or a specific title in good condition, a book dealer may be the best resource.

Magazines

Fishing and outdoors magazines represent one of the most important links between angling's past and present for collectors. By reading the articles, first-person accounts, how-to stories, editorials,

Tying on a fly

This classic angling image of a fly fisherman tying on a fly appeared on the cover of a 1935 L. L. Bean catalog.

Fishing art

The art of fishing was never more beautifully illustrated than on the covers of vintage sporting magazines and tackle manufacturers' catalogs. From leaping trout to hungry northern pike, fish and fishing were recreated with the colorful enthusiasm of a bygone era on famous magazines such as Outdoor Life, Sports Afield, *and* Field & Stream, *as well as the Pflueger tackle catalog. "Fish and feel fit!" was a famous slogan of the day from the famed South Bend Bait Company. This selection of cover art is from the collection of Pete Press.*

and advertisements found in old magazines, collectors can follow the evolution of fishing, as well as research various collectibles. Vintage magazines reveal how anglers viewed various innovations at the time of their introduction and provide valuable information about when specific products gained popularity. In some cases, magazines, along with catalogs, hold the key to unlocking mysteries associated with the manufacturing and release dates of tackle.

Fishing and outdoors publications began appearing in the 1800s. The first to regularly address outdoor sports in the United States was the *American Turf Register and Sporting Magazine*, which started circulation in 1829. Gradually, other sporting periodicals like the *Spirit of the Times* followed, until the market boomed in the latter half of the nineteenth century. Publications such as the *Fishing Gazette*, the *American Angler*, and *Forest and Stream* fed a hungry audience of anglers eager to learn how to improve their tactics, read thrilling accounts of other anglers' adventures, and discover the latest advancements in tackle technology.

Still-popular publications like *Outdoor Life* and *Sports Afield* were born in the outdoors magazine boom of the late 1800s. Such magazines acted as a link that connected the anglers of North America. Without leaving home, an angler living in Ohio went along on a fly-fishing trip to Montana, or a New York angler traveled to Florida to catch monster bass. Fishing magazines informed, entertained, and put the average angler in touch with the experts. They helped popularize the sport and fueled the trend of anglers traveling to other parts of the continent to sample the diverse fishing opportunities that they had read about in their favorite magazines. The periodicals also pushed conservation issues into the national spotlight with editorial discussions and helped lay the foundation for early game-management legislation.

Smoky Mountain trout fishing

This postcard illustration shows an angler on a trout stream in Great Smoky Mountains National Park.

The now-famous anglers who wrote about their adventures or secret tactics are another prize old fishing publications offer to the collector. Anglers such as Theodore Gordon, Lee Wulff, and Zane Grey shared their expertise with the public through magazines, and some of their best writing survives only in the pages of old outdoors publications. To own a magazine with one of those rare stories is to own a valuable piece of angling and literary history.

Along with the classic writing that appears in old fishing periodicals are wonderful illustrations and photographs that helped

Go-Ite catalog cover

The Go-Ite Manufacturing Company hailed from Detroit, Michigan.

bring life to the stories. Colorful cover illustrations of fishing scenes and striking black-and-white photographs of anglers displaying their prize catches were typical of the artwork found in turn-of-the-century fishing and outdoors publications. The photographs represent valuable bookmarks in the evolution of the sport. They preserve a moment in angling history and reveal otherwise unknown details about the sport's equipment and the anglers that used it. The illustrated covers are now a lost art because most fishing magazines long ago replaced cover illustrations with color photographs. Today, the exciting scenes once portrayed by illustrators of anglers battling fish or of trophy fish taking bait are classic pieces of angling artwork and are highly collectible.

Fortunately for collectors, many old fishing and outdoors publications are available at reasonable prices. Since anglers tend to save magazines, thousands upon thousands of copies of famous and not-so-famous publications remain in circulation. Finding a copy of a magazine with the cover intact is not always easy, nor is finding a specific issue, but antique stores and flea markets commonly carry a healthy selection of old fishing magazines in various states of wear. With a little searching, collectors can usually find the copies they want, but the age and circulation of the magazine play key roles in its availability. Finding the first issue of *Field & Stream* from 1896 is probably unlikely, while copies of *Sports Afield* from the 1930s may be abundant.

Collectors who want to research vintage fishing and outdoors magazines can save time and money by visiting a public library. Quite often libraries carry copies of old publications on microfilm or can help track down copies at other libraries. When researching early publications it is important to note that magazines have not always used the cataloging or page-numbering format used by today's publications. Publishers commonly numbered their magazines by volume rather than issue, and numbered advertising pages independently from the rest of the magazine. Although the numbering systems are confusing, one helpful feature that many old magazines offer is an advertising index at the front or back of the publication, which provides a quick reference to the ads and their page numbers.

Catalogs

Long before the advent of radio and television, commercial tackle manufacturers relied on catalogs as their most important means of advertising. The earliest catalogs from the mid-1800s were simple and often dull lists of products, but as competition in the tackle industry boomed in the late 1800s, manufacturers realized they needed a new approach to make their products more attractive to anglers. At first, companies added cover art, sketches, and descriptions of products, but that was not enough. Looking for new ways to reach out to consumers, companies commissioned color artwork for their catalog covers. They included tips on how to use tackle, and

Pocket catalog

Pocket catalogs like this one issued by Pflueger in 1938 are highly collectible pieces of angling memorabilia. Tackle companies often packaged pocket catalogs with lures and reels, hoping anglers could be enticed to buy additional products from the company.

"Good Fishing!"

The first lesson at Lou Eppinger's School of Fly and Bait Casting probably instructed students to buy a healthy supply of Dardevles in all colors and sizes.

even paid famous outdoorsmen to write articles or endorsements. Lively descriptions of products made each item sound like the most fantastic advancement the sport had ever seen, and companies backed up those descriptions with angler testimonials.

Like magazines, catalogs were both entertaining and educational. They kept anglers abreast of the latest advancements in tackle and provided information on how they could improve their performance on the lake or stream. Catalogs remain an important means of advertising today, but with ever-increasing advertising opportunities through cable and satellite television and the Internet, the catalog has lost the advertising power it once had. Some companies still depend heavily on catalogs, while others use them only to supplement other forms of advertising.

For collectors, catalogs hold a double value. Not only are they valuable pieces of angling memorabilia, but they also act as identification tools. Collectors often encounter problems accurately dating and identifying antique tackle, but by referencing old catalogs, they acquire valuable information about their pieces, such as model names, model variations, and years of production. Likewise, they can date innovations in the trade and follow tackle's evolution. Catalogs also provide valuable facts on the histories of different tackle companies, possibly including the details of a company's background or a list of personnel—information that may not be available through any other source.

Collectors often try to track down catalogs that include tackle they own to see how a company advertised a specific lure, rod, or reel and to read the colorful descriptions of those products. For instance, if a collector that owns a Heddon Dowagiac Minnow from 1923 finds a Heddon catalog from that year, a whole new dimension to owning that lure has been added. The catalog contains the original advertisement for the lure, which provides a description of it, the price, and the colors it came in. It also gives the collector some insight into the company's style of advertising and reveals information on the other products sold by Heddon that year.

As mentioned earlier, a catalog's illustrations played an important role in grabbing the consumer's attention. Paintings and sketches of anglers battling large fish grace the covers of many of these publications. Not only are they classic portrayals of the sport, they also represent a wonderful advertising hook that consciously and subconsciously told consumers that they too could catch trophy fish if they bought the products inside.

Creek Chub catalog

Company catalogs play an instrumental role as research tools for collectors. Inside this Creek Chub catalog is important information about the lures and tackle the company produced in 1935, including the specific colors and styles of its products.

Collectors who try to track down catalogs soon discover that there are four different types. The most popular is the company retail catalog, which consumers received in the mail. It includes the company's line of tackle, descriptions, and prices, as well as entertaining or informative tidbits. Companies also distributed wholesale catalogs to retailers. Sometimes the wholesale catalogs looked nearly identical to the retail catalogs, but in other cases they included additional information about their products. In their never-ending attempt to capture the angler's attention, manufacturers also packaged pocket catalogs with their lures, rods, and reels. The pocket versions usually contained incomplete information on a company's products and have limited research value to today's collector because manufacturers commonly issued the same pocket catalogs for more than one year and did not date them. The fourth type of catalog was not issued by the manufacturer, but instead by retailers. Companies received additional exposure by selling their products secondhand through mail-order company catalogs like Sears, Roebuck, and Company. These catalogs varied widely in their format and may or may not contain valuable identification information.

Finding old fishing catalogs can be rather easy, because people often saved them just as they save magazines, but finding a specific catalog is another matter. The age and the number of catalogs produced by a company in a specific year are key factors in their availability, as is the level of demand from catalog collectors. Finding catalogs in good or excellent condition can also be difficult, because they have often spent decades sitting in attics, garages, or basements and are water damaged, ripped, bent, or faded. In many cases, collectors are happy just to find one with a cover and all the pages intact.

Trade Signs

Catalogs proved an efficient means of advertising tackle and fishing gear through the mail, but tackle companies discovered long ago that they needed a different strategy to sell their products in bait and sporting-goods stores. In order to make certain items attractive to anglers, dealers needed a way to grab customers' attention when they were strolling through the aisles of the store. Early on in the commercial tackle trade, manufacturers came up with the idea of in-store promotion. Usually, these advertisements were signs dealers hung on their walls or displays that they assembled and placed on the floor or counter. In-store advertisements could be as simple as a colorful illustrated poster or as complex as a giant, plastic reproduction of a lure. The gimmicks that manufacturers have used as advertisements through the years range from the ludicrous to the beautiful, but regardless of their artistic merits, most are valuable collectibles today.

Unfortunately for collectors, dealers commonly discarded in-store advertisements when a promotion ended in order to make room for the next promotional piece. In most cases, only a handful of examples of these displays survive, and those that are available,

Fishing sells

Other industries joined tackle companies in using fishing scenes to sell products. Beer and cigarette companies such as the Minneapolis Brewing Company and the R. A. Patterson Tobacco Company of Richmond, Virginia, also used illustrations and photographs of fishing to promote their products, which included Grain Belt beer and Lucky Strike cigarettes. Countless other companies, such as the ones pictured here, used images of fishing in their marketing campaigns. From makers of cars to candy, they all seemed to find fishing as common ground. Some of the signs and posters they produced rival those created by tackle companies and are in high demand by collectors of fishing, beer, and cigarette memorabilia.

No "medical" plugs—
No "fancy" lures—
Just the world's best tobacco...

For a TREAT
instead of a TREATMENT
smoke Old Golds

IT'LL BE <u>MORE</u> FUN
"GETTING THERE"

There's a *Ford* in your future!

Long trips, short trips—even an after-dinner spin around the block —they're all going to be more fun when peace brings your new Ford car. ... For your coming Ford will be big and roomy, too. Rich looking—inside and out—its smart lines will surely rate a

"second look" on street and highway. ... Naturally, this new car will live up to the famous Ford tradition for economy and reliability. Into it will go all the skill and experience that Ford has gained in more than 40 years.

... When? We're going to start production plans as soon as we receive the

necessary "go ahead." Meanwhile, the full Ford resources will continue to be engaged in helping speed the Victory.

FORD MOTOR COMPANY

especially the unusual examples, carry high price tags.

The advertising signs produced by companies are not the only type of signs collectors pursue. The business signs from old bait stores also have found a following in the world of fishing collectibles. In most cases, these signs are one-of-a-kind. Hand-carved and painted wooden signs like those created by renowned decoy-carver Oscar Peterson are extremely rare. Collectors have found only a handful of his bait-store signs, but the search goes on for others that he reportedly produced.

Calendars

To help advertise their products, tackle manufacturers and beer companies often distributed calendars depicting various fishing scenes. Companies like the Horton Manufacturing Company of Bristol, Connecticut, which owned Bristol Rods, and the Winchester Repeating Arms Company of New Haven, Connecticut, produced beautiful calendars in the early decades of the 1900s. To make their calendars stand out from the rest, some companies commissioned reputable artists to provide the illustrations. The use of stone lithography created wonderfully vivid colors that rival even the best modern reproduction techniques. The results of their advertising efforts stand as extraordinary examples of fishing art.

Many fishing calendars, especially those created around the turn of the century, are quite rare today. The original owner often discarded the calendar at the end of the year or ripped off pages with each passing month, making finding these calendars, and finding them intact, very difficult. Occasionally, however, collectors stumble upon that uncommon gem tucked away in some attic or storeroom, which is in good condition and intact from January to December.

The scope of collectible fishing art and literature is limited only by the depths to which a collector is willing to dig. Other collectible items include fishing regulations books, matchbook covers, post cards, carved or mounted fish, sculptures, postage stamps, and brochures, but these items represent just a handful of the fishing art and literature available.

As the river of time drifts along, collectors will continue to pull new and exciting finds from its waters. They will wade upstream, casting and hoping for that next bite, which could be a lure no one else has found. In the whisper of the water washing over the riffles they will hear the distant voices of men like Heddon and Orvis who walked the river long before, testing their products, which grew to become the objects of angling legend. The river is long and deep and so are the possibilities.

Facing page: **A boy and his stringer of fish**

Fishing calendars can be one of the toughest collectibles to find intact. Owners often ripped pages off at the end of the month or discarded their calendars at the end of the year, making it difficult to find surviving prints like this one from 1942.

Appendix

Collectors' Resources

American Fish Decoy Association
624 Merritt Street
Fife Lake, MI 49633-9142
(616) 879-3912

The American Museum of Fly Fishing
P.O. Box 42
Manchester, VT 05254
(802) 362-3300
www.amff.com

The Antique Outboard Motor Club, Inc.
Department IN
P.O. Box 69
Sussex, WI 53089
www.aomci.org

Florida Antique Tackle Collectors
P.O. Box 420703
Kissimmee, FL 34742-0703
www.fatc.net

Granville Island Sport Fishing Museum
1502 Duranleau
Granville Island
Vancouver, BC
Canada V6H 3S4
(604) 683-1939
www.sportfishingmuseum.bc.ca

Great Lakes Fish Decoy Collectors
& Carvers Association
35824 W. Chicago
Livonia, MI 48150
(734) 427-7768

The International Hunting and Fishing Museum
P.O. Box 1028
Williamston, NC 27892-1028
(252) 809-1795
www.ihfm.org

The Meisselbach Association
14099 Lakeshore Drive
Nampa, ID 83686

The Michigan Lure Collectors Club
P.O. Box 79
Lennon, MI 48449

National Fishing Lure Collectors Club
HCR #3
P.O. Box 4012
Reeds Springs, MO 65737
(417) 338-4427
www.nflcc.com

National Freshwater Fishing Hall of Fame
Box 33 Hall of Fame Drive
Hayward, WI 54843
(715) 634-4440
www.freshwater-fishing.org

The Old Reel Collectors Association
160 Shoreline Walk
Alpharetta, GA 30022
(770) 521-1877
www.orcaonline.org

Bibliography

Some of the sources used in researching this book include:

Brooks, Joe. *Trout Fishing*. New York: Outdoor Life, 1972.

Calabi, Silvio. *The Collector's Guide To Antique Fishing Tackle*. Secaucus, NJ: The Wellfleet Press, 1989.

Koller, Larry. *The Treasury of Angling*. New York: Golden Press, 1963.

Kewley, Charles, and Howard Farrar. *Fishing Tackle For Collectors*. London; New York: Sotheby's Publications, 1987.

Liu, Allan J., ed. *The American Sporting Collector's Handbook*. Tulsa, OK: Winchester Press, 1982.

Luckey, Carl F. *Old Fishing Lures and Tackle*. 2d ed. Florence, AL: Books Americana, 1986.

Murphy, Dudley, and Rick Edmisten. *Fishing Lure Collectibles*. Paducah, KY: Collector Books, 1995.

Tonelli, Donna. *Top of the Line Fishing Collectibles*. Atglen, PA: Schiffer Publishing, Ltd., 1997.

Vernon, Steven K. *Antique Fishing Reels*. Harrisburg, PA: Stackpole Books, 1985.

Above: **Postcard** *circa* **1940**

Index